WORKBOOK for

MICROSOFT
Office 2000

Introductory Concepts and Techniques

WORD 2000   EXCEL 2000   ACCESS 2000   POWERPOINT 2000   OUTLOOK 2000

Gary B. Shelly
Thomas J. Cashman
Timothy J. Walker

Contributing Author
David T. Nuscher

COURSE TECHNOLOGY
ONE MAIN STREET
CAMBRIDGE MA 02142

Thomson Learning™

SHELLY
CASHMAN
SERIES.

Australia • Canada • Denmark • Japan • Mexico • New Zealand • Philippines
Puerto Rico • Singapore • South Africa • Spain • United Kingdom • United States

Microsoft Office 2000
Introductory Concepts and Techniques
Workbook

CONTENTS

Microsoft Outlook 2000

Microsoft Integration 2000

PREFACE

T his Workbook is intended as a supplement to *Microsoft Office 2000: Introductory Concepts and Techniques* by Gary Shelly, Thomas Cashman, and Misty Vermaat. A variety of activities are provided in a format that is easy to follow and facilitates learning the material presented by helping students recall, review, and master introductory Microsoft Office 2000 concepts and techniques.

Each project in the Workbook includes:

- An **Overview** summarizing the project's content and containing a partial Chapter Outline designed to be completed by the students. The Chapter Outline helps students identify, organize, and recognize relationships between important concepts.
- A **Review** that assists students in assessing their mastery of the subject matter through Matching, True/False, Definition, Screen Identification, Dialog Box, Multiple Choice, Fill in the Blanks, Sequence, and Short Answer questions.
- **Activities** calculated to help students develop a deeper understanding of the information in each project through Use Help exercises, Expanding on the Lab exercises, and a Puzzle that supplies a more entertaining approach to reviewing important terms and concepts.

In addition to the activities in each project, the Workbook also offers a To the Student section that provides tips on using the textbook effectively, attending class, preparing for and taking tests, and using the Workbook.

Acknowledgments

The Shelly Cashman Series would not be the leading computer education series without the contributions of outstanding publishing professionals. First, and foremost, among them is Becky Herrington, director of production and designer. She is the heart and soul of the Shelly Cashman Series, and it is only through her leadership, dedication, and tireless efforts that superior products are made possible. Becky created and produced the award-winning Windows series of books.

Under Becky's direction, the following individuals made significant contributions to these books: Doug Cowley, production manager; Ginny Harvey, series specialist and developmental editor; Ken Russo, senior Web designer; Mike Bodnar, associate production manager; Stephanie Nance, graphic artist and cover designer; Mark Norton, Web designer; Meena Mohtadi, production editor; Marlo Mitchem, Chris Schneider, Hector Arvizu, Kenny Tran, and Dave Bonnewitz, graphic artists; Jeanne Black and Betty Hopkins, Quark experts; Nancy Lamm, Lyn Markowicz, Margaret Gatling, and Laurie Sullivan, copyeditors; Marilyn Martin, Kim Kosmatka, Cherilyn King, Mary Steinman, and Pat Hadden proofreaders; Cristina Haley, indexer; Sarah Evertson of Image Quest, photo researcher; and Susan Sebok and Ginny Harvey, contributing writers.

Special thanks go to Richard Keaveny, managing editor; Jim Quasney, series consulting editor; Lora Wade, product manager; Erin Bennett, associate product manager; Francis Schurgot, Web product manager; Marc Ouellette, Associate Web Product manager; Scott Wiseman, online developer; Rajika Gupta, marketing manager; and Erin Runyon, editorial assistant.

Gary B. Shelly
Thomas J. Cashman
Timothy J. Walker

TO THE STUDENT

W ould you like to be promised success in this course? Your textbook, *Microsoft Office 2000: Introductory Concepts and Techniques*, can be a source of the knowledge you will need to excel. Unfortunately, no textbook alone can guarantee mastery of the subject matter. To a great extent, genuine understanding depends on how hard you are willing to work. There are other resources available, however, that can help you to get the most out of this course. That is the intent of this Workbook.

Following are tips on using the textbook, attending class, preparing for and taking tests, and using this Workbook. Most of the tips in the first three areas will not only help to improve your performance in this course, they also can be applied to many of your other classes. The tips in the last area are designed to explain how this Workbook can enhance your understanding of the material in *Microsoft Office 2000: Introductory Concepts and Techniques*.

Using the Textbook

The textbook is one of your most important tools in building a solid foundation in the subject matter. To use your textbook most effectively, follow these guidelines:

Survey the whole textbook first. The table of contents supplies an overview of the topics covered in the textbook. The preface explains the textbook's goals, objectives, pedagogical approach, organization, and student activities. As you scan the textbook, see how projects are arranged, the way key terms and concepts are indicated, where illustrations and tables are used, and the types of exercises that conclude each project. Look for special features interspersed throughout the textbook and check how the index can be used to clarify information.

Start by skimming the project. Study the project objectives, which identify what you are expected to learn. Read the project introduction and the Case Perspective, which give you a general idea of the project's content. Next, skim the project. Look at the section headings to get a feeling for how sections are related to each other. Notice bold or italic text; usually, these words are important. Finally, read the brief summary at the end of the chapter. The summary restates, in broad terms, the major concepts and conclusions offered in the project.

Carefully read the entire project. Some instructors prefer that you only skim a project before class and then do a detailed reading after their lecture. Other instructors want you to read the project thoroughly before class. Whenever you sit down to read the entire project, it may help first to review the exercises at the end of the project to provide a more specific focus for your reading. Read the two-page briefs that introduce each project in *Microsoft Office 2000: Introductory Concepts and Techniques*. As you read through the rest of the project, make sure you understand all of the key terms and concepts. Pay particular attention to illustrations (screens, diagrams, and tables) and their captions; often, they help clarify ideas in the text. Write in your textbook — highlight important points, note relationships, and jot questions. Study the More Abouts that are scattered throughout each project. Thoughtfully examine the summary material (What You Should Know). If there is anything you do not remember or understand, go back and reread the relevant sections. Do the guided exercise that builds on the material presented in the project (Apply Your Knowledge). Finally, complete any assigned additional exercises (In the Lab, Cases and Places).

Attending Class

Attending class is a key ingredient for success in a course. Simply showing up, however, is not enough. To get the most out of class, follow these guidelines:

Arrive early and prepared. Sit close enough to the front of the room so that you can hear well and see any visual materials, such as slides or transparencies, clearly. Make sure you have necessary supplies, such as a notebook, writing implement, and your textbook. Be ready to start when your instructor begins.

Take notes. For most people, note-taking is essential to recall later the material presented in class. Note-taking styles vary: some people just jot down keywords and concepts, while others write more detailed narratives. The important thing is that the style you adopt works for you. If, when you later consult your notes, you find they do little to help you remember the subject of the lecture, try to be more comprehensive. If you find that in taking notes you frequently fall behind your instructor, try to be more brief. Many people review their notes as soon as possible after class, fleshing them out while the material is still fresh.

Do not be afraid to ask questions. Often, people hesitate to ask questions because they fear they will appear foolish. In reality, asking good questions is a sign of intelligence; after all, you have to be insightful enough to realize something is unclear. Keep in mind that frequently your classmates have the same questions you do. Good questions not only can help clarify difficult topics, they also increase the depth of your understanding by suggesting relationships between ideas or establishing the impact of concepts. Learn the best time to ask questions. In small classes, sometimes it is possible to ask questions during a lecture. In a larger setting, it may be best to approach your instructor after class or to make an appointment. If you feel really lost, your instructor may be able to recommend a peer tutor or an academic counseling service to help you.

Preparing for and Taking Tests

Tests are an opportunity for you to demonstrate how much you have learned. Many strategies are proven to improve performance on tests. To do your best on a test, follow these guidelines:

Find out as much as you can about the test. Ask your instructor what material will be covered, what types of questions will be used, how much time you will have, and what supplies you will need (pencil or pen, paper or bluebook, calculator, perhaps even notes or a textbook if it is an open-book test). You will be more likely to do your best work if there are no surprises. Occasionally, copies of previous tests are available. These are invaluable aids in test preparation.

Use your resources wisely. Start studying by reviewing your notes and, in *Microsoft Office 2000: Introductory Concepts and Techniques*, by reviewing the What You Should Know section at the end of each project. Review carefully and attempt to anticipate some of the questions that may be asked. Reread sections in your textbook on topics you are not sure of or that seem especially important. Try to really comprehend, and not merely memorize, the material. If you truly understand a concept, you no doubt will be able to answer any question, regardless of the type. Understanding often makes remembering easier. For example, if you know how font size is measured, it is simple to recall the font sizes commonly used in documents and worksheets. When memorizing is necessary, use whatever techniques work best for you (memory tricks, verbal repetition, flash cards, and so on).

Avoid cramming. To prepare for an athletic contest, you would not practice for twelve straight hours before the event. In the same way, you should not expect to do well on a test by spending the entire night before cramming. When you cram, facts become easily confused, and anything you do to keep them straight probably will be remembered only for a short time. It also is difficult to recognize how concepts are related, which can be an important factor in successful test taking. Try to study in increments over a period of time. Use the night before the test to do a general review of the pertinent material, concentrating on what seems most difficult. Then, get a good night's sleep so you are well rested and at your best when it is time for the test.

Take time to look through the test. Arrive early enough at the test site to get properly settled. Listen for any special instructions that might be given. Skim the entire test before you start. Read the directions carefully. You may not need to answer every question in each section, or you may have to answer some questions in a certain way. Determine the worth of each part, the parts you think can be done most quickly, and the parts you believe will take the longest to complete. Use your assessment to budget your time.

Answer the questions you are sure of first. As you work through the test, read each question carefully and answer the easier ones first. If you are not certain of an answer, skip that question for now, ensuring you get the maximum number of "sure" points and guaranteeing less worry about time when dealing later with the more difficult questions. Occasionally, you will find the information you needed to answer one of the questions you skipped can be found elsewhere in the test. Other times, you suddenly will remember what you need to answer a question you skipped as you are dealing with another part of the test.

Use common sense. Most questions have logical answers. While these answers often require specific knowledge, sometimes it is possible to determine a correct answer with a general grasp of the subject matter and a little common sense. When you go back over the test after you are finished, make sure your answers are reasonable. Do not change an answer, however, unless you are sure your first answer was wrong. If incorrect answers are not penalized any more than having no answer at all, it is better to try a logical guess than to leave an answer blank. But, if you are penalized for incorrect answers (for example, if your final score is the number of correct answers minus the number of incorrect answers), you will have to decide whether or not to answer a question you are not sure of based on how confident you are of your guess.

✎ Using this Workbook

The purpose of this Workbook is to further your understanding of the concepts presented in *Microsoft Office 2000: Introductory Concepts and Techniques*. Each Workbook project should be completed *after* you have finished the corresponding project in the textbook. The Workbook projects are divided into sections, each of which has a specific purpose:

Overview. This section provides a brief summary of the project's content and a Project Outline. Use the Overview to recall the general information in the project. The Project Outline is a partially completed outline of the project, along with the page numbers on which important topics can be found in the text. The Project Outline is designed not only to help you review the material, but also to assist you in organizing and seeing the relationships between concepts. Complete the Project Outline in as much depth as you feel is necessary. Because your completions should be meaningful to you, they may be different from a classmate's. You can refer directly to the textbook as you work through the outline while rereading the chapter, or you can fill in the outline on your own and then use the textbook to check the information you have supplied. When entering the steps necessary to perform a task, think in general, rather than specific, terms. For example, "Type the worksheet title" is a better completion than "Type Fun-N-Sun Sojourn 1st Qtr Sales."

Review. This is a tool you can use to evaluate your mastery of the chapter. The Review consists of several different types of questions: Matching, True/False, Definitions, Screen Identification, Multiple Choice, Fill in the Blanks, Dialog Box, Sequence, and Short Answer. Try to complete the Review without referring to your textbook or notes. Leave any answer you are unsure of blank or, if you prefer, guess at the answer but indicate you were unsure by placing a question mark (?) after your response. When you have finished the Review, use *Microsoft Office 2000: Introductory Concepts and Techniques* to check your answers. Correct any answers that were incorrect or uncertain. If necessary, ask your instructor to explain any concepts or techniques that still are unclear.

Activities. These are things you can do to reinforce and expand on the concepts presented in each project. Use Help asks you to employ various types of Microsoft Office Help to learn more about topics presented in the project. Expanding on the Lab extends your work with one of the project lab exercises. Finally, the Puzzle is designed to review important terms in an entertaining fashion by offering definitions or descriptions and asking you to complete different types of puzzles by supplying the associated terms.

Essential
Introduction to Computers

Overview

This introduction presents basic concepts associated with computers and their use. You learn why computers and application software are studied, what a computer is, what a computer does, and how a computer knows what to do. The components of a computer are described including: input devices, the central processing unit, memory, output devices, and auxiliary storage. You discover how system software is different from application software and become acquainted with the purpose of some application software packages. Networks, the Internet, and the World Wide Web are introduced. Finally, you find out how to purchase, install, and maintain a personal computer.

Project Outline

I. Why study computers and application software? [COM2]

Today, many people feel that knowing how to use a computer is a basic skill necessary to succeed in business and to function effectively in society.

II. What is a computer? [COM3]

A computer is _an electronic device for storing + processing data, typically in binary form, according to instructions given to it in a variable program_

III. What does a computer do? [COM3]

All computers perform the information processing cycle, which is comprised of four general operations:

- _Input_
- _Process_
- _output_
- _storage_

These operations describe the procedures a computer performs to process data into information and store it for future use.

Data refers to _is a set of values of qualitative/quant variables_

Information is _facts provided or learned_

Computer users are _person who uses computers_

IV. How does a computer know what to do? [COM4]

A computer program is _sequence of instructions, written to perform a specific task w/ a computer_

Once the program is stored, the computer executes one instruction after another until the job is complete.

V. What are the components of a computer? [COM4]

The four primary components of a computer are: _Central processing unit_ _RAM, motherboard, hard drive_

A. Input devices [COM5]

Input devices are _computer hardware used to provide data + control signals to the computer_

The two primary input devices are the keyboard and the mouse.

1. The keyboard [COM5]

The keyboard is _used to enter data into a computer_

An enhanced keyboard consists of _12 function keys not 10_

2. The mouse [COM6]

A mouse is _hard operated electronic device that controls the cursor_

B. The central processing unit [COM7]

The central processing unit (CPU) contains _arithmetic/logic unit, control unit, & registers_

The CPU is made up of the control unit and the arithmetic/logic unit.

- The control unit interprets _instructions & control subsequent behavior_
- The arithmetic/logic unit performs _integer arithmetic + logical operations_

A microprocessor is _a chip that contains a CPU._

C. Memory [COM7]

Memory consists of _instructions & data that your computers microprocessor can reach quickly._

The amount of memory typically is measured in kilobytes or megabytes.

- One kilobyte (K or KB) ≈ _1,024 bytes_
- One megabyte (M or MB) ≈ _1,040,576 bytes_

A byte, or memory location, usually stores _8 bits_

D. Output devices [COM7]

Output devices make _hard copy of any information that could be displayed on a monitor_

Two commonly used output devices are printers and monitors.

1. Printers [COM7]

An impact printer prints by _banging a head or needle against an ink ribbon to make the mark_

One type of impact printer used with personal computers is the dot matrix printer.

Nonimpact printers form characters by _inkjet = spray small drops_

laser = roll ink onto paper using cylinder drum

- Ink-jet printers form _____

  _____

- Laser printers work _____

  _____

2. Computer screens [COM9]

A screen, monitor, or CRT is _device that displays signals on a computer screen._

Liquid crystal display (LCD) is _allows displays to be much thinner than cathode ray tube tech_

Pixels are _physical point in a raster image_

E. Auxiliary storage [COM10]

Auxiliary storage devices , also called secondary storage devices, are _____

Addressable data storage that is not currently in a

Types of auxiliary storage used on personal computers are floppy disks, hard disks, CD-_comp memory_

ROMs, and DVD-ROMs.

1. Floppy disks [COM10]

A floppy disk is _storage medium composed of disk of thin flexible magnetic storage medium, sealed in plastic_

The most widely used floppy disk is _zip drive_

A floppy disk drive is _where you insert floppy disk_

Most magnetic disks are read/write storage media, meaning _files can be executed directly_

Formatting is _appearance + presentation_

- A track is _concentric rings at a constant radius_
- A sector is _angular blocks_

Access time is _84 milliseconds_

2. Hard disks [COM11]

A hard disk consists of _____

_____

Typical hard disk sizes range from 6 GB to 19 GB.

- A gigabyte (GB) ≈ _____

3. CD-ROMs [COM12]

CD-ROMs (compact disk read-only memory) are _____

_____

CD-ROMs often are used for multimedia material.

Multimedia combines _____

4. DVD-ROMs [COM12]

A DVD (digital video disc-ROM) is _____

_____

VI. Computer software [COM13]

Computer software is the key to productive use of computers.

A. System software [COM13]

System software consists of _____

_____

The operating system, an important part of system software, tells _____

_____

A graphical user interface (GUI) provides _____

_____

DOS (Disk Operating System) is _____

B. Application software [COM13]

Application software consists of _____

_____

VII. Personal computer application software [COM14]

A. Word processing software [COM14]

Word processing software is _____

_____

B. Spreadsheet [COM14]

Electronic spreadsheet software allows _____

_____

C. Database [COM14]

Database software allows _____

_____

D. Presentation graphics [COM15]

Presentation graphics software allows _____

_____

VIII. Networks and the Internet [COM15]

A network is _____

_____

- A local area network (LAN) is _____

_____

- A wide area network (WAN) is _____

_____

A. The Internet [COM16]

The Internet is _____

_____

125 million people use the Internet for:

- _____
- _____
- _____
- _____
- _____

Most users connect to the Internet in one of two ways:

- An Internet service provider (ISP) is _____

_____

- An online service provides _____

_____

B. The World Wide Web [COM17]

The World Wide Web is _____

_____

A Web page is _____

_____

A Web site is _____

A Web browser is _____

A Uniform Resource Locator (URL) is _____

The domain name identifies _____

A Web server is _____

IX. How to purchase, install, and maintain a personal computer [COM18]

    A. How to purchase a personal computer [COM18]

        1. _____

        2. _____

        3. _____

        4. _____

        5. _____

        6. _____

        7. _____

        8. _____

        9. _____

       10. _____

       11. _____

       12. _____

       13. _____

    B. How to purchase a laptop computer [COM23]

        1. _____

        2. _____

        3. _____

        4. _____

        5. _____

        6. _____

        7. _____

        8. _____

        9. _____

    C. How to install a personal computer [COM25]

        1. _____

        2. _____

        3. _____

        4. _____

        5. _____

        6. _____

        7. _____

        8. _____

        9. _____

       10. _____

11. _____

12. _____

13. _____

14. _____

15. _____

D. How to maintain a personal computer [COM28]

1. _____

2. _____

3. _____

4. _____

5. _____

6. _____

7. _____

Review

Matching (5)

Match each term on the left with the best description from the right.

____ 1. input devices

____ 2. central processing unit

____ 3. memory

____ 4. output devices

____ 5. auxiliary storage devices

a. make(s) the information resulting from processing available for use

b. store(s) instructions and data while they are not being processed

c. convert(s) a computer's digital signals into analog signals that can be sent over telephone lines

d. contain(s) the electronic circuits that cause processing to occur

e. store(s) data – including numbers, letters, graphics, and sound – while it is being processed

f. link(s) a limited geographical area, such as a school computer laboratory or group of buildings

g. allow(s) data, programs, commands, and user responses to be entered into a computer

True/False (10)

*Circle **T** if the statement is true and **F** if the statement is false.*

T   F   1. All computer processing requires data.

T   F   2. The control unit performs the logical and arithmetic processes.

T   F   3. A computer with 64 MB of memory can store 32,000 pages of text information.

T   F   5. Impact printers do a better job printing different fonts and are quieter.

T   F   6. Although hard disks are available in fixed cartridge form, most hard disks can be removed from the computer.

T   F   7. Because of their small storage capacity, CD-ROMs seldom are used for multimedia material.

T   F   8. The different ways people use computers in their careers or in their personal lives are examples of application software.

T   F   9. Some software packages, such as Microsoft Office 2000, also include access to the World Wide Web as an integral part of the application.

T   F   10. When buying a computer system, use cash to purchase your system.

Definitions (5)

Briefly define each term.

1. end user _____

2. microprocessor _____

3. booting _____

4. http:// (hypertext transfer protocol) _____

5. computer virus _____

Personal Computer Devices (10)

Identify the devices that comprise the personal computer in Figure COM1, and note the operation(s) in the information processing cycle (input, process, output, or storage) for which they are used.

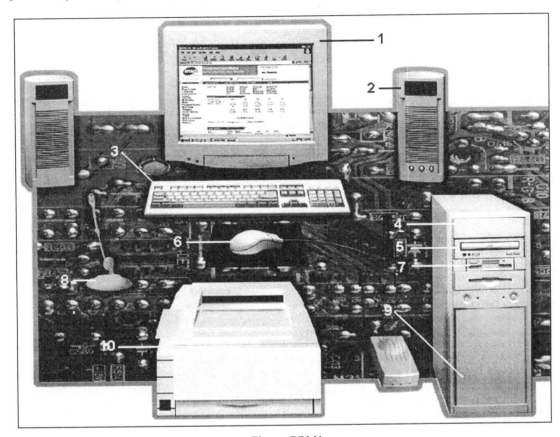

Figure COM1

Device	Information Processing Operation(s)
1. _____	_____
2. _____	_____
3. _____	_____
4. _____	_____
5. _____	_____
6. _____	_____
7. _____	_____
8. _____	_____
9. _____	_____
10. _____	_____

Multiple Choice (5)

Circle the letter of the best answer.

1. During what operation in the information processing cycle is the information created put into some form, such as a printed report or color graphics?
    a.   input
    b.   process
    c.   output
    d.   storage

2. Which of the following is *not* a type of nonimpact printer?
    a.   dot matrix printer
    b.   ink-jet printer
    c.   laser printer
    d.   all of the above

3. Today, what is the size and capacity of the most widely used floppy disks?
    a.   5.25 inches and 720 kilobytes of storage
    b.   3.5 inches and 720 kilobytes of storage
    c.   5.25 inches and 1.44 megabytes of storage
    d.   3.5 inches and 1.44 megabytes of storage

4. Which of the following has the greatest storage capacity?
    a.   floppy disks
    b.   hard disks
    c.   CD-ROMs
    d.   DVD-ROMs

5. Which of the following is *not* a guideline for purchasing a personal computer?
    a.   determine what application products you will use on your computer
    b.   consider just price
    c.   look for free software
    d.   be aware of hidden costs

Fill in the Blanks (5)

Write a word (or words) in the blank to correctly complete each sentence.

1. The goal of _____ is to incorporate comfort, efficiency, and safety into the design of items in the workplace.

2. _____, which is an application that combines text and graphics, uses laser printers to produce high-quality black-and-white or color output.

3. When discussing a storage medium, the term _____ means you can remove the medium from one computer and carry it to another computer.

4. Computers are networked together so users can share _____, such as hardware devices, software programs, data, and information.

5. _____ your hard disk reorganizes files so they are in contiguous (adjacent) clusters, making disk operations faster.

Understanding the Keyboard (5)

Identify the numbered areas on the keyboard in Figure COM2.

Figure COM2

1. _____   4. _____

2. _____   5. _____

3. _____

Sequence (5)

Use the numbers 1 – 5 to show the order in which these steps are performed by a laser printer.

____   A set of rollers uses heat and pressure to fuse the toner permanently to the paper.

____   The laser beam creates a charge that causes toner to stick to the drum.

____   As the drum continues to rotate and press against the paper, toner is transferred from the drum to the paper.

____   The drum rotates as gears and rollers feed a sheet of paper into the printer.

____   A rotating mirror deflects a low-powered laser beam across the surface of a drum.

Short Answer (5)

Write a brief answer to each question.

1. How are dot matrix printers different from ink-jet printers and laser printers? What advantages do nonimpact printers have over impact printers?

2. How is a floppy disk different from a hard disk?

3. How is system software different from application software? Why is a graphical user interface (GUI) important?

4. Why do people use the Internet? How is an Internet service provider (ISP) different from an online service?

5. What are diagnostic tools? How can diagnostic tools be obtained?

Activities

Expanding on the Lab

Use Figure COM3 to determine guidelines for the ideal work area. Under My Work Area, check Yes or No depending on whether your work area meets the specified guidelines.

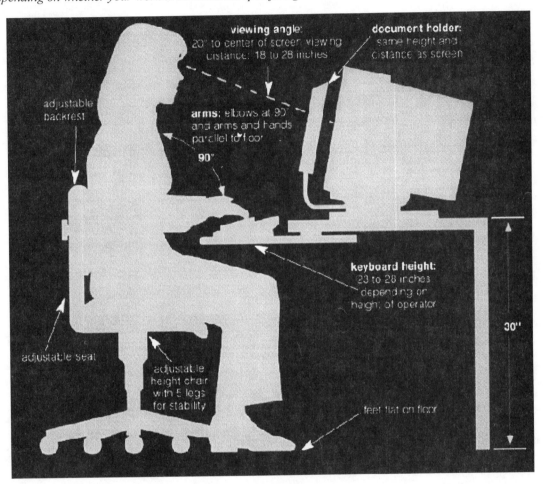

viewing angle:
20° to center of screen; viewing distance: 18 to 28 inches

document holder:
same height and distance as screen

adjustable backrest

arms: elbows at 90° and arms and hands parallel to floor

90°

keyboard height:
23 to 28 inches depending on height of operator

adjustable seat

adjustable height chair with 5 legs for stability

feet flat on floor

30"

Figure COM3

Work Area Guidelines	My Work Area			
Chair				
_____ backrest	☐	Yes	☐	No
_____ seat	☐	Yes	☐	No
_____ height	☐	Yes	☐	No
_____ legs for stability	☐	Yes	☐	No
Arms				
elbows at _____	☐	Yes	☐	No
arms and hands _____	☐	Yes	☐	No

Work Area Guidelines	My Work Area
Viewing angle _____ to center of the screen viewing distance _____ inches	☐ Yes ☐ No ☐ Yes ☐ No
Horizontal height _____ inches desktop height _____ inches	☐ Yes ☐ No ☐ Yes ☐ No
Document holder same height and distance as screen	☐ Yes ☐ No

Would you give your work area a "Passing" or "Failing" grade. Why? _____

_____

Puzzle

Use the clues below to complete the word search puzzle. Words in the puzzle may be forward or backward, across, up and down, or diagonal.

Introduction to Computers

```
R  K  R  O  W  T  E  N  U  A  ■  T  R  T  E
R  O  T  C  E  S  L  ■  T  P  U  A  E  E  T
D  U  S  E  R  S  B  C  ■  P  C  I  T  J  Y
V  ■  C  S  ■  L  A  N  N  L  G  D  U  K  B
D  E  I  K  E  P  T  I  A  I  N  E  P  N  A
R  D  M  S  M  C  R  ■  W  C  I  M  M  I  G
O  R  O  I  N  F  O  R  M  A  T  I  O  N  I
M  A  N  D  T  E  P  R  L  T  T  T  C  T  G
O  O  O  Y  O  S  R  A  P  I  A  L  S  E  N
N  B  G  P  ■  U  S  A  M  O  M  U  L  R  I
I  Y  R  P  M  E  T  E  W  N  R  M  E  N  T
T  E  E  O  R  A  M  P  C  T  O  C  X  E  O
O  K  R  L  D  O  ■  ■  U  C  F  K  I  T  O
R  D  C  F  R  K  C  A  R  T  A  O  P  M  B
C  D  ■  Y  ■  U  H  A  R  D  D  I  S  K  ■
```

Accepts data, manipulates it according to rules stored in its memory unit, produces information, and stores the results.

Raw facts given to the computer during the input operation.

Data that is organized, has meaning, and is useful.

People who use a computer directly or use the information it provides.

Detailed set of instructions that tell a computer what to do.

Type of devices that allow data, programs, commands, and user responses to be entered into a computer.

Commonly used input device on which data is entered by typing.

Science that incorporates comfort, efficiency, and safety into workplace design.

Contains the electronic circuits that cause processing to occur.

Small chip into which a personal computer CPU is designed.

Electronic components that store data during processing; also called RAM.

Memory location that usually stores one character.

Type of devices that make the information resulting from processing available for use.

Television-like display device.

Type of printer that prints by striking an inked ribbon against the paper.

Type of printer that forms characters by other means than striking a ribbon against paper.

Popular and affordable type of printer that forms a character by spraying drops of ink onto the page.

Type of printer that works similarly to a copying machine.

Flat panel technology similar to a digital watch.

Individual picture elements that make up the surface of a computer screen.

Portable, inexpensive storage medium consisting of a flexible disk with a magnetic coating.

Describes storage medium that can be removed from one computer and carried to another.

Process of preparing a floppy disk for reading and writing by organizing the disk into storage locations.

Narrow recording band that forms a full circle on the surface of a disk.

Small arc on a disk track, capable of storing 512 bytes of data.

Period required to find and retrieve data.

One or more rigid platters coated with a metal oxide material that allows data to be stored magnetically.

One billion bytes.

Discs used to store large amounts of prerecorded information.

Combines text, graphics, animation, video, and audio.

High capacity compact disc capable of storing a telephone book for the entire United States.

Process of loading the operating system into the computer's memory.

Type of software that tells a computer how to produce information.

Collection of computers and devices connected via communications media and devices.

Network that covers a limited geographic area such as an office.

Network that covers a large geographic area such as the district offices of a national corporation.

The world's largest network.

Unique address of a Web page.

Microsoft Windows 98 and Office 2000

Project One
An Introduction to Windows 98 and Office 2000

Overview

This project illustrates the Microsoft Windows 98 graphical user interface and the Microsoft Office 2000 applications. You start Windows 98, learn the components of the desktop, and master the six mouse operations. You open, close, move, resize, minimize, maximize, and scroll a window. Windows Explorer is used to select and copy a group of files, display the contents of a folder, create a folder, expand and collapse a folder, and rename and delete a file and a folder. You discover how to obtain help about using Microsoft Windows 98. You learn how to shut down Windows 98. Brief explanations of the Microsoft Office 2000 applications and examples of how these applications interact with the Internet, World Wide Web, and intranets are given. With this introduction you are ready to begin a more in-depth study of each Microsoft Office 2000 application explained in this book.

Project Outline

I. Introduction [INT 1.4]

Microsoft Windows 98 is _____

_____

Microsoft Office 2000 is _____

_____

II. What is Microsoft Windows 98? [INT 1.5]

An operating system is _____

_____

Microsoft Windows 98 is _____

Features of Windows 98:

- Windows 98 is called a 32-bit operating system because _____

_____

- Windows 98 includes Microsoft Internet Explorer (IE), which is _____

_____

- Windows 98 is compatible with all existing application programs, which are _____

_____

A. What is a user interface? [INT 1.5]

A user interface is _____

_____

The goal of an effective user interface is to be user friendly, meaning _____

_____

A graphical user interface (GUI) is _____

_____

B. Launching Microsoft Windows 98 [INT 1.6]

After the computer is turned on and the introductory Microsoft Windows 98 screen clears,

several items display on a background called the _____

Items on the desktop include nine icons and their titles:

- My Computer allows you to _____
- My Documents allows you to _____
- Internet Explorer allows you to _____
- Network Neighborhood allows you to _____
- Recycle Bin allows you to _____
- The Microsoft Network allows you to _____
- My Briefcase allows you to _____
- Online Services allows you to _____
- Microsoft Outlook allows you to _____

The taskbar at the bottom of the screen contains:

- The Start button allows you to _____

_____

- The Quick Launch toolbar contains _____

_____

- The taskbar button area contains _____

_____

- The tray status area contains _____

_____

A Welcome to Windows 98 screen may display on the desktop.

On the desktop, the mouse pointer is _____

_____

Nearly every item on the Windows 95 desktop is considered an object. Every object has

properties, which are _____

C. Closing the Welcome screen [INT 1.8]

☞ To close the Welcome screen

1. _____

D. The desktop as a work area [INT 1.8]

You may think of the Windows desktop as _____

_____

III. Communicating with Microsoft Windows 98 [INT 1.8]

You can request information or respond to messages using either a mouse or the keyboard.

A. Mouse operations [INT 1.8]

A mouse is _____

The primary mouse button is _____

The secondary mouse button is _____

Using the mouse, you can perform the following operations: point, click, right-click, double-click, drag, and right-drag.

B. Point and click [INT 1.9]

Point means _____

_____

Click means _____

☞ To point and click

1. _____

A ScreenTip is _____

2. _____

The Start menu contains_____

A menu is _____

A command directs _____

• A right arrow indicates _____

• An ellipses indicates _____

3. _____

The Programs submenu contains_____

A submenu is _____

4. _____

C. Right-click [INT 1.11]

Right-click means _____

☞ To right-click

    1. _____

       A shortcut menu contains _____

    2. _____

    3. _____

D. Double-click [INT 1.13]

Double-click means _____

_____

☞ To open a window by double-clicking

    1. _____

The active window is _____

E. My Computer window [INT 1.14]

The My Computer window shows what is on your computer.

The window border determines _____

The title bar contains _____

The menu bar is _____

The Standard Buttons toolbar contains _____

_____

The area below the Standard Buttons toolbar contains:

  • drive icons _____

  • folders _____

The status bar contains_____

F. Minimize button [INT 1.14]

When you click the Minimize button _____

_____

☞ To minimize and redisplay a window

    1. _____

    2. _____

    3. _____

G. Maximize and Restore button [INT 1.16]

The Maximize button is used to _____

The Restore button replaces _____

☞ To maximize and restore a window

    1. _____

    2. _____

       The Undo button allows you to _____

The Delete button allows you to _____

The Properties button allows you to _____

The Views button allows you to _____

3. _____

4. _____

H. Close button [INT 1.19]

The Close button closes _____

☞ To close a window and reopen a window

1. _____

2. _____

3. _____

I. Drag [INT 1.20]

Drag means _____

_____

☞ To move an object by dragging

1. _____

2. _____

J. Sizing a window by dragging [INT 1.21]

☞ To size a window by dragging

1. _____

The up scroll arrow, down scroll arrow, and scroll box on the vertical scroll bar enable you to

_____

K. Scrolling in a window [INT 1.22]

Scrolling can be accomplished in three ways:

1. _____

2. _____

3. _____

☞ To scroll a window using scroll arrows

1. _____

2. _____

3. _____

L. Resizing a window [INT 1.24]

☞ To resize a window

1. _____

2. _____

M. Closing a window [INT 1.24]

☞ To close a window

1. _____

2. _____

3. _____

N. Right-drag [INT 1.24]

Right-drag means _____

_____

☞ To right-drag

1. _____

2. _____

3. _____ .

Shortcut menu commands:

• Cancel will _____

• Move Here is used to _____

• Copy Here will _____

• Create Shortcut(s) Here allows you to _____

O. Summary of mouse and Windows operations [INT 1.26]

_____

IV. The keyboard and keyboard shortcuts [INT 1.26]

The keyboard is _____

Many tasks you accomplish with a mouse also can be accomplished using keyboard shortcuts.

Keyboard shortcuts consist of:

1. _____

For example, press F1 to _____

2. _____

For example, press CTRL+ESC to _____

V. The Windows 98 desktop views [INT 1.27]

Windows 98 provides three desktop views:

• The Classic style causes _____

_____

• In Web style, the icon titles are _____

_____

• The Custom style is _____

_____

VI. Launching an application program [INT 1.27]

A program is _____

An application program is _____

A Web browser program is _____

Microsoft Internet Explorer is a widely used Web browser.

A. Launching an application using the Start button [INT 1.27]

One method to launch an application program is to use the Start menu.

☞ To launch a program using the Start menu

1. _____

The Internet Explorer command on the Internet Explorer submenu launches Internet Explorer.

2. _____

B. Quitting a program [INT 1.29]

☞ To quit a program

1. _____

2. _____

VII. Windows Explorer [INT 1.30]

Windows Explorer is _____

_____

Windows Explorer can be used to:

1. _____

2. _____

3. _____

4. _____

A. Starting Windows Explorer and maximizing its window [INT 1.30]

☞ To start Windows Explorer and maximize its window

1. _____

2. _____

B. The Exploring – My Computer window [INT 1.31]

When you start Windows Explorer by right-clicking the My Computer icon, Windows 98 opens the Exploring – My Computer window. The window is divided into two panes. The left pane, called the Folders pane, contains a hierarchy, or ranked arrangement, of folders on the computer. The right pane, called the Contents pane, shows the contents of the highlighted folder in the Folders pane.

Each folder on the All Folders side is represented by _____

A minus sign (-) is displayed to the left of an icon in the Folders pane to indicate _____

_____

Subfolders are _____

Collapsing the folder by clicking the minus sign removes _____

_____

A plus sign (+) is displayed to the left of an icon in the Folders side to indicate _____

_____

Expanding the folder by clicking the plus sign displays _____

_____

If neither a plus sign nor a minus sign displays _____

_____

The status bar at the bottom of the window indicates _____

_____

C. Displaying the contents of a folder [INT 1.33]

  ☞ To display the contents of a folder

    1. _____

    2. _____

D. Expanding a folder [INT 1.35]

  ☞ To expand a folder

    1. _____

    2. _____

E. Collapsing a folder [INT 1.36]

  ☞ To collapse a folder

    1. _____

    2. _____

VIII. Copying files to a folder on a floppy disk [INT 1.37]

Copying a file or a group of files from one disk to another or from one folder to another is a common operation. When copying files:

• The source drive and source folder are _____

_____

• The destination drive and destination folder are _____

_____

A. Creating a new folder [INT 1.37]

☞ To create a new folder

1. _____

2. _____

3. _____

4. _____

5. _____

6. _____

B. Displaying the destination folder [INT 1.40]

Prior to copying files, the destination folder must be visible in the Folders pane, and the files

to be copied must be visible in the Contents pane.

☞ To expand a folder

1. _____

2. _____

C. Displaying the contents of the Windows folder [INT 1.40]

☞ To display the contents of a folder

1. _____

2. _____

3. _____

D. Changing the view [INT 1.42]

The Contents pane can be displayed in Large Icons, Small Icons, List, or Details view.

• In large icons view _____

• In list view _____

☞ To change to list view

1. _____

2. _____

E. Selecting a group of files [INT 1.43]

To copy a single file _____

_____

Group files are copied in a similar fashion, except that the entire group is selected in the

Contents pane.

☞ To select a group of files

1. _____

2. _____

3. _____

F. Copying a group of files [INT 1.45]

☞ To copy a group of files

1. _____

2. _____

3. _____

4. _____

A dialog box displays _____

G. Displaying the contents of the My Files folder [INT 1.46]

☞ To display the contents of a folder

1. _____

2. _____

H. Renaming a file or folder [INT 1.47]

For various reasons, you may wish to change the name of a file or folder.

☞ To rename a file

1. _____

2. _____

3. _____

☞ To rename a folder

1. _____

2. _____

3. _____

IX. Deleting a file or folder [INT 1.49]

When a file or folder on the hard drive is deleted, Windows 98 temporarily stores the deleted file in the Recycle Bin until the Recycle Bin is emptied. When a file of folder on a floppy disk is deleted, however, the file or folder is *deleted immediately.*

A. Deleting a file by right-clicking its file name [INT 1.49]

☞ To delete a file by right-clicking

1. _____

2. _____

3. _____

B. Deleting a folder [INT 1.51]

☞ To delete a folder

1. _____

2. _____

3. _____

4. _____

C. Quitting Windows Explorer [INT 1.52]

☞ To quit a program

1. _____

2. _____

X. Using Windows Help [INT 1.52]

Windows Help is available when _____

_____

A. Contents sheet [INT 1.52]

The Contents sheet involves _____

_____

☞ To launch Windows Help

1. _____

2. _____

On the Contents sheet:

A closed book icon indicates _____

A question mark icon indicates _____

☞ To use Help to find a topic in Help

1. _____

2. _____

3. _____

4. _____

Help toolbar buttons:

- Hide button _____

- Back button or Forward button _____

- Options button _____

- Web Help button _____

B. Index sheet [INT 1.56]

The Index sheet lists _____

_____

☞ To use the Help Index sheet

1. _____

2. _____

3. _____

☞ To close Windows Help

    1. _____

XI. Shutting down Windows 98 [INT 1.58]

The Shut Down command on the Start menu is used to _____

☞ To shut down Windows 98

    1. _____

    2. _____

    3. _____

If you accidentally click Shut Down on the Start menu and you do not want to shut down

Windows 98, click _____

XII. What is Microsoft Office 2000? [INT 1.59]

Microsoft Office 2000 is _____

_____

Microsoft Office 2000 Premium Edition includes _____

_____

Microsoft Office 2000 includes:

- A clip art gallery with images, sounds, photographs, animations, themes, and backgrounds.

- Menus and toolbars that adjust to the way you work.

- Self-repairing applications.

- Applications integrated with the power of the Internet.

A. The Internet, World Wide Web, and Intranets [INT 1.60]

The Internet is _____

_____

The World Wide Web is _____

_____

- A Web site can consist of _____

_____

- A Uniform Resource Locator (URL) identifies _____

- Web servers are _____

- A browser, such as Microsoft Internet Explorer, is _____

_____

- A hyperlink is _____

An intranet is _____

_____

B. Microsoft Office 2000 and the Internet [INT 1.60]

Microsoft Office 2000 allows users to utilize the Internet or an intranet as a central location to view documents, manage files, and work together. Each Office 2000 application makes publishing documents on a Web server as simple as saving a file on a hard disk.

XIII. Microsoft Word 2000 [INT 1.61]

Microsoft Word 2000 is _____

_____

A. Microsoft Word 2000 and the Internet [INT 1.62]

Microsoft Word makes it possible to _____

_____

XIV. Microsoft Excel 2000 [INT 1.63]

Microsoft Excel 2000 is _____

_____

A. Microsoft Excel 2000 and the Internet [INT 1.63]

Using Microsoft Excel 2000, you can _____

_____

XV. Microsoft Access 2000 [INT 1.64]

Microsoft Access 2000 is _____

A database is _____

A. Microsoft Access 2000 and the Internet [INT 1.65]

Databases provide _____

_____

XVI. Microsoft PowerPoint 2000 [INT 1.66]

Microsoft PowerPoint 2000 is _____

_____

A. Microsoft PowerPoint 2000 and the Internet [INT 1.66]

PowerPoint allows you to _____

_____

XVII. The Web toolbar [INT 1.68]

The Web toolbar allows you to _____

_____

XVIII. Microsoft Publisher 2000 [INT 1.69]

Microsoft Publisher 2000 is _____

_____

Microsoft Publisher can be used to design camera ready publications, which means _____

_____

A. Microsoft Publisher and the Internet [INT 1.70]

Microsoft Publisher allows _____

_____

XIX. Microsoft FrontPage 2000 [INT 1.70]

Microsoft FrontPage 2000 is _____

_____

XX. Microsoft PhotoDraw 2000 [INT 1.71]

Microsoft PhotoDraw 2000 is _____

_____

XXI. Microsoft Outlook 2000 [INT 1.72]

Microsoft Outlook 2000 is _____

_____

XXII. The Microsoft Office 2000 Help system [INT 1.74]

While using Microsoft Office, several categories of help are available. One of the easiest methods to obtain help is the Office Assistant. The Office Assistant answers _____

_____

Review

Matching (5)

Match each term on the left with the best description from the right.

___ 1. Microsoft Word 2000

___ 2. Microsoft Excel 2000

___ 3. Microsoft Access 2000

___ 4. Microsoft PowerPoint 2000

___ 5. Microsoft Outlook 2000

a. a spreadsheet program that allows you to organize data, perform calculations, make decisions, and graph data

b. a flexible drawing program that you can use to create, edit, and view pictures, and even edit scanned photos

c. a full-featured word processing program that allows you to create many types of communications

d. an integrated desktop information management program that helps you organize and share information

e. a comprehensive database program that allows you to add, change, sort, and retrieve data and create reports

f. a complete presentation graphics program that allows you to produce professional-looking presentations

g. an extensive file-management program that allows you to see and manipulate the files and folders

True/False (10)

*Circle **T** if the statement is true and **F** if the statement is false.*

T F 1. Hardware alone forms the user interface.

T F 2. Research studies have indicated that the use of graphics can play an important role in aiding users to interact effectively with a computer.

T F 3. A minimized window is not open but it does display on the screen.

T F 4. The size of the scroll box in any window is dependant on the amount of the window that is visible; that is, the smaller the scroll box, the more of the window that is visible.

T F 5. When you start Windows Explorer by right-clicking the My Computer icon, Windows 98 opens the Exploring – My Briefcase window.

T F 6. If neither a plus sign (+) nor a minus sign (-) displays to the left side of an icon in the Folders pane of the Exploring window, the folder does not contain subfolders.

T F 7. The contents of the folder you click in the Folders pane of the Exploring window will display in the Contents pane of the window.

T F 8. To rename a folder, double-click the folder name, type the new folder name, and then press the ENTER key.

T F 9. Microsoft Office 2000 allows you to take advantage of the Internet, World Wide Web, and intranets.

T F 10. The Office Assistant and balloon display whenever you start any Microsoft 2000 application.

Definitions (5)

Briefly define each term.

1. icon _____

2. title bar _____

3. subfolder _____

4. clip art file _____

5. hyperlink _____

The Windows 98 Screen (5)

Identify the elements indicated in Figure INT1.

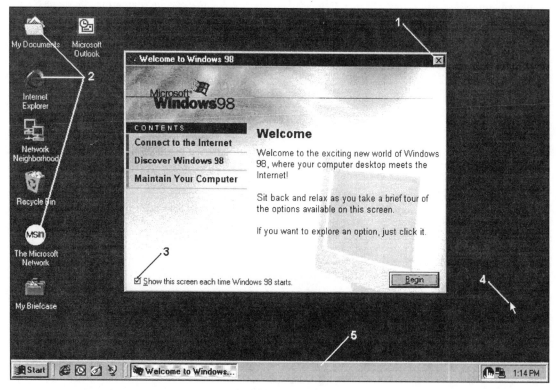

Figure INT1

1. _____   4. _____

2. _____   5. _____

3. _____

Multiple Choice (5)

Circle the letter of the best answer.

1. For what purpose is the My Briefcase icon on the Windows 98 desktop used?
   a. to connect to and browse the Internet
   b. to work with other computers connected to your computer
   c. to receive and send e-mail
   d. to transfer documents and folders to and from a portable computer

2. What is *not* a way that you can scroll in a window?
   a. click the scroll arrows
   b. click the scroll bar
   c. drag the scroll arrows
   d. drag the scroll box

3. When the Exploring – My Computer window is opened, what is indicated on the status bar at the bottom of the window?
   a. the number of folders, or objects, displayed in the Folders pane of the window
   b. the names of folders and subfolders in the Folders pane of the window
   c. the number of folders, or objects, displayed in the Contents pane of the window
   d. the names of folders and subfolders in the Contents pane of the window

4. How do you select a group of files in the Contents pane of the Exploring window?
   a. click the first file name, and then hold down the CTRL key and click the remaining file names
   b. click the first file name, and then hold down the ALT key and click the remaining file names
   c. click the first file name, and then hold down the HOME key and click the remaining file names
   d. click the first file name, and then hold down the TAB key and click the remaining file names

5. What Microsoft Office 2000 application would you use to create and manage professional-looking Web sites on the Internet or an intranet?
   a. Microsoft PowerPoint 2000
   b. Microsoft Publisher 2000
   c. Microsoft FrontPage 2000
   d. Microsoft PhotoDraw 2000

Shortcut Menu (5)

Answer the following questions about the shortcut menu shown in Figure INT2.

Figure INT2

1. How was the shortcut menu displayed? _____

2. What submenu is displayed? _____

3. What folder's content is displayed in the Contents pane? _____

4. In what view is the Contents pane? _____

5. If List is clicked, how will the Contents pane display? _____

_____

Fill in the Blanks (5)

Write a word (or words) in the blank to complete each sentence correctly.

1. The goal of an effective user interface is to be _____, meaning that the software can be used easily by individuals with limited training.

2. Clicking the icon on the left of a window title bar will open the _____, which contains commands to carry out actions associated with the window.

3. In the My Computer window, each button on the Standard Buttons toolbar contains a(n) _____ and an icon describing its function.

4. The left frame of the Windows Help window contains three _____, Contents, Index, and Search.

5. The first page in a Web site is called the _____ and is identified by a unique address, called a Uniform Resource Locator (URL).

Sequence (5)

Use the numbers 1 – 5 to show the order in which these steps should be performed to create a new folder using Windows Explorer.

____ In the Folders pane, click the name of the folder in which the new folder will be created.

____ Point to Folder on the New submenu.

____ Type the new folder name in the text box and then press the ENTER key.

____ Click Folder on the New submenu.

____ Right-click an open area of the Contents pane and then point to New on the shortcut menu.

Short Answer (5)

Write a brief answer to each question.

1. How are commands followed by an ellipsis (…) different from commands followed by a right arrow (▶)?

2. How is right-dragging different from dragging? Why is right-dragging the safest way to drag?

3. When are computer users more likely to use keyboard shortcuts instead of the mouse? What is the keyboard shortcut to start Help?

4. How is deleting a file or folder from the hard drive different from deleting a file or folder from a floppy disk?

5. Why is the Web toolbar the easiest method to navigate an intranet or the Internet?

Activities

Use Help

Use Help to answer each question.

1. When using Windows Help, how can you **print a topic**? Using the Introducing Windows 98 book on the Contents sheet, look in the How to Use Help book to find out.

2. How can you **reverse mouse buttons**? Use the Index sheet to find out.

3. What keyboard shortcuts are available **for Windows Explorer only**? Using the Exploring Your Computer book on the Contents sheet, look in the Keyboard Shortcuts book to find out.

Expanding on the Lab

Perform the following tasks.

1. Open the Exploring – My Computer window. Expand the Hard disk (C:) folder. Display the contents of the Windows folder.

2. Right-click the Black Thatch file name in the Contents pane. Click Properties on the shortcut menu to display the properties of the file.

3. Note the Type, Location, Size, and MS-DOS name of the Black Thatch file.

4. Click the Cancel button to close the Properties dialog box.

5. Find a file with the same icon as Black Thatch. Right-click the file name and click Properties on the shortcut menu to display the properties of the file.

6. List the properties of the file that are the same as the properties of Black Thatch. List the properties that are different.

7. Click the Cancel button in the Properties dialog box.

8. Find a file with an icon that is different from Black Thatch. Right-click the file name and click Properties on the shortcut men to display the properties of the file.

9. List the properties of the file that are the same as the properties of Black Thatch. List the properties that are different.

10. Click the Cancel button in the Properties dialog box. Close all open windows.

Puzzle

Use the clues given to complete the crossword puzzle.

Windows 98 and Office 2000

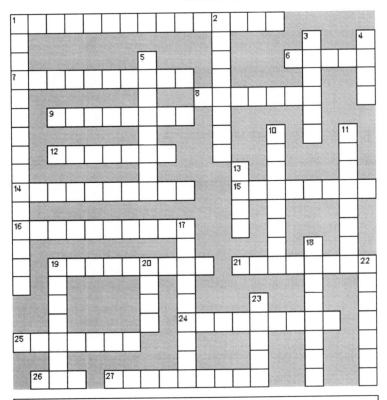

Down

1. Instructions that control hardware allocation and provide the capability of communicating with a computer.
2. Contains a small icon and the window title.
3. Drive or folder containing files to be copied.
4. List of related commands.
5. Button that removes a window from the desktop and displays a non-recessed button for the window on the taskbar.
10. Start menu command used to turn off Windows 98.
11. Worldwide network of thousands of computer networks.
13. View in which files are arranged in columns and each file is represented by a smaller icon.
17. Located at the bottom of a window.
18. Input device on which data is manually typed.
19. Button that replaces the Maximize button when a window is maximized.
20. Point to an item, hold down the primary mouse button, move the item, and release the mouse button.
22. Menu that displays when pointing to a command followed by a right arrow.
23. Press and release the primary mouse button.

Across

1. Answers questions and suggests more efficient ways to complete tasks.
6. Pointing device attached to the computer by a cable.
7. Press and release the secondary mouse button.
8. Contains a list of menu names.
9. Button that enlarges a window so it fills the entire screen.
12. Style that causes the desktop and objects on it to display and function as in Windows 95.
14. Opens when the icon at the left on the window title bar is clicked.
15. Type of Web available only to users of a particular type of computer network.
16. Folders indented and aligned below a folder name in the Folders pane.
19. Point to an item, hold down the secondary mouse button, move the item, and release the mouse button.
21. Help sheet used to browse through topics by category.
24. Can be dragged to view areas of a window that are not currently visible.
25. Set of computer instructions that carries out a task on the computer.
26. Style in which icon titles on the desktop are underlined and can be clicked.
27. Colored or underlined text that connects to another Web page.

Microsoft Word 2000

Project One
Creating and Editing a Word Document

This project introduces starting Word and using the Word window to create a document. Before entering any text in the document, you learn how to change the font size. As you enter text, you learn about formatting marks, Wordwrap, spell checker, and scrolling. Once the document is saved, you format paragraphs and characters in the document. Next, you insert a graphic, and center and resize it. You also discover how to save and print a document, quit Word, and open a document. With the technologies presented, you learn to move the insertion point so you can insert, delete, and modify text. Finally, you find out how to use the Word Help system.

Project Outline

   I.   What is Microsoft Word 2000? [WD 1.6]

      Microsoft Word is _____

      _____

  II. Project One – Summit Peak Announcement [WD 1.6]

 III. Starting Word [WD 1.8]

      ☞ To start Word:

          1. _____

             A highlighted command displays _____

          2. _____

             _____

          3. _____

          4. _____

             _____

 IV. The Word window [WD 1.9]

      The Word window consists of _____

      _____

A. Document window [WD 1.9]

The document window is _____

_____

Main elements of the Word document window:

1. Insertion point [WD 1.10]

The insertion point is _____

_____

2. End mark [WD 1.10]

The end mark is _____

_____

3. Mouse pointer [WD 1.11]

The mouse pointer becomes _____

_____

4. Rulers [WD 1.11]

The horizontal ruler is _____

_____

The vertical ruler sometimes displays _____

_____

5. Scroll bars [WD 1.11]

Scroll bars are used to _____

_____

The scroll box reflects _____

_____

6. Status bar [WD 1.11]

The status bar presents _____

_____

Status indicators are used to _____

_____

A ScreenTip is _____

_____

B. Menu bar and toolbars [WD 1.11]

1. Menu bar [WD 1.12]

The menu bar displays _____

•   A short menu lists _____

- A full menu lists _____

  A hidden command _____

  An unavailable command _____

2. Toolbars [WD 1.12]

   Toolbars contain _____

   _____

   - A docked toolbar is _____

     To display an entire toolbar, double-click its move handle, which is _____

     _____

     When you click a toolbar's More Buttons button, Word displays _____

     _____

   - A floating toolbar is _____

C. Resetting menus and toolbars [WD 1.14]

   ☞ To reset my usage data and toolbar buttons [MO C.1]

      1. _____

      2. _____

         _____

      3. _____

         _____

      4. _____

         _____

      5. _____

D. Displaying the entire Standard toolbar [WD 1.14]

   ☞ To display the entire Standard toolbar

      1. _____

E. Zooming page width [WD 1.15]

   The zoom page width command is used to _____

   _____

   ☞ To zoom page width

      1. _____

      2. _____

      3. _____

      4. _____

V. Changing the default font size [WD 1.16]

   The font defines _____

The default (preset) font is _____

Font size specifies _____

A single point is _____

☞ To increase the default font size before typing

    1. _____

       _____

    2. _____

VI. Entering text [WD 1.17]

☞ To enter text

    1. _____

       _____

    2. _____

    3. _____

The Spelling and Grammar Status icon displays _____

_____

The Spelling and Grammar status icon shows:

An animated pencil (✐) as _____

A red check mark (✓) if _____

A red X (✗) if _____

A. Entering blank lines into a document [WD 1.19]

☞ To enter blank lines into a document

    1. _____

B. Displaying formatting marks [WD 1.20]

A formatting mark is _____

_____

   • The paragraph mark (¶) shows _____

   • A raised dot (•) shows _____

☞ To display formatting marks

    1. _____

       _____

    2. _____

C. Entering more text [WD 1.21]

☞ To enter more text

    1. _____

    2. _____

    3. _____

D. Using wordwrap [WD 1.21]

Wordwrap allows _____

_____

Press the ENTER key only in these circumstances:

    1. _____

    2. _____

    3. _____

    4. _____

  ☞ To wordwrap text as you type

     1. _____

E. Checking spelling automatically as you type [WD 1.22]

A red wavy underline displays if _____

A green wavy underline displays if _____

  ☞ To check spelling as you type

     1. _____

     2. _____

     3. _____

     4. _____

If a flagged word is spelled correctly, click _____

F. Entering text that scrolls the document window [WD 1.24]

As you enter more lines of text than Word can display in the document window, Word scrolls the top portion of the document upward off the screen.

  ☞ To enter text that scrolls the document window

     1. _____

The scroll box indicates _____

VII. Saving a document [WD 1.26]

Any document that will be used later must be saved.

  ☞ To save a new document

     1. _____

     2. _____

     A folder is _____

     3. _____

     4. _____

     5. _____

VIII. Formatting paragraphs and characters in a document [WD 1.29]

- Paragraph formatting is _____

_____

- Character formatting is _____

_____

A. Selecting and formatting paragraphs and characters [WD 1.29]

To format a single paragraph, position the insertion point in the paragraph and then format it.

To format multiple paragraphs or words, the paragraphs or words first must be selected.

Selected text is _____

B. Selecting multiple paragraphs [WD 1.30]

☞ To select multiple paragraphs

1. _____

_____

2. _____

C. Changing the font of selected text [WD 1.30]

☞ To change the font of selected text

1. _____

_____

2. _____

D. Changing the font size of selected text [WD 1.31]

☞ To change the font size of selected text

1. _____

_____

2. _____

3. _____

E. Bold selected text [WD 1.32]

Bold characters display thicker than those that are not bold.

☞ To bold selected text

1. _____

F. Right-align a paragraph [WD 1.33]

Default paragraph alignment is left-aligned, that is _____

_____

A right-aligned paragraph is _____

_____

☞ To right-align a paragraph

1. _____

2. _____

G. Center a paragraph [WD 1.34]

To center a paragraph is to position the paragraph horizontally between the left and right margins on the page.

☞ To center a paragraph

1. _____

H. Undoing commands or actions [WD 1.35]

- The Undo button can be used to _____

- The Redo button can be used to _____

☞ To undo an action

1. _____
_____

2. _____

I. Selecting a line and formatting it [WD 1.36]

☞ To select a line

1. _____
_____

☞ To format a line of text

1. _____
_____

2. _____

J. Selecting a word [WD 1.37]

☞ To select a word

1. _____

2. _____

K. Italicize selected text [WD 1.39]

☞ To italicize selected text

1. _____

L. Scrolling [WD 1.39]

☞ To scroll through the document

1. _____

2. _____

☞ To center a paragraph

1. _____

2. _____

   M. Selecting a group of words [WD 1.40]

     ☞ To select a group of words

       1. _____

       2. _____

   N. Underlining selected text [WD 1.41]

     ☞ To underline selected text

       1. _____

          _____

 IX. Inserting clip art into a Word document [WD 1.42]

   Graphics are _____

   Clip art is _____

   Clip art is located in the Clip Gallery, which contains _____

   _____

   A. Inserting clip art [WD 1.43]

   ☞ To insert clip art into a document

       1. _____

          _____

       2. _____

       3. _____

       4. _____

       5. _____

       6. _____

          _____

   B. Selecting and centering a graphic [WD 1.46]

   ☞ To select a graphic

       1. _____

          _____

         A selection rectangle surrounds the graphic, with small squares, or sizing handles, at each corner and middle location.

   ☞ To center a selected graphic

       1. _____

   C. Resizing a graphic [WD 1.47]

   Resizing includes _____

   ☞ To resize a graphic

       1. _____

2. _____

_____

3. _____

D. Restoring a resized graphic to its original size [WD 1.48]

To restore a resized graphic to its exact original size, click _____

_____

X. Saving an existing document with the same file name [WD 1.48]

☞ To save an existing document with the same file name

1. _____

_____

XI. Printing a document [WD 1.49]

A hard copy or printout is _____

☞ To print a document

1. _____

_____

2. _____

XII. Quitting Word [WD 1.50]

☞ To quit Word

1. _____

2. _____

XIII. Opening a document [WD 1.51]

☞ To open a document

1. _____

2. _____

_____

3. _____

XIV. Correcting errors [WD 1.53]

Changes to a document can be required because the document contains an error or because of new circumstances.

A. Types of changes made to documents [WD 1.53]

1. Additions [WD 1.53]

_____

2. Deletions [WD 1.53]

_____

3. Modifications [WD 1.53]

_____

A. Inserting text into an existing document [WD 1.54]

☞ To insert text into an existing document

1. _____

2. _____

- In insert mode _____

- In overtype mode _____

Double-click the OVR status indicator on the status bar to switch to overtype mode.

B. Deleting text from an existing document [WD 1.54]

☞ To delete an incorrect character in a document

1. _____

2. _____

☞ To delete an incorrect word or phrase in a document

1. _____

2. _____

_____

C. Closing the entire document [WD 1.54]

☞ To close the entire document and start over

1. _____

2. _____

3. _____

XV. Word Help system [WD 1.55]

The Word Help system can be used to _____

_____

A. Using the Office Assistant [WD 1.55]

The Office Assistant answers _____

_____

The Office Assistant is part of Word's IntelliSense technology.

☞ To obtain Help using the Office Assistant

1. _____

_____

2. _____

3. _____

_____

    4. _____

☞ To quit Word

    1. _____

Review

Matching (5)

Match each term on the left with the best description from the right.

___ 1. scroll bar
___ 2. menu bar
___ 3. toolbar
___ 4. status bar
___ 5. title bar

a. used to set tab stops, indent paragraphs, and change page margins

b. displays the document title

c. presents names that represent lists of commands

d. where text and graphics display

e. contains buttons, boxes, and menus that are used to perform tasks quickly

f. located at the bottom of the screen

g. used to display different portions of a document in the document window

True/False (10)

*Circle **T** if the statement is true and **F** if the statement is false.*

T   F   1. The insertion point is a short horizontal line that indicates the end of your document.

T   F   2. The Standard and Formatting toolbars are preset to display as floating toolbars in the document window.

T   F   3. If Word 2000 is installed on a new computer the default font size and font is 10 point Arial.

T   F   4. In general, if all of the words you have typed are in Word's dictionary and your grammar is correct, the Spelling and Grammar icon displays a red check mark.

T   F   5. As you enter text using Word, press the ENTER key whenever you reach the right margin.

T   F   6. To conceal the wavy underlines that mark possible spelling errors, right-click the Spelling and Grammar Status icon and then click Hide Spelling Errors on the shortcut menu.

T   F   7. You can use either the mouse or the keyboard to scroll through a document.

T   F   8. When formatting text, paragraphs encompass the text up to, but not including, the paragraph mark (¶).

T   F   9. When a graphic is selected, the Picture toolbar displays automatically on the screen.

T   F   10. When resizing a graphic, if you have a precise measurement, drag the resizing handles; otherwise, use the Format Picture dialog box.

Definitions (5)

Briefly define each term.

1. document window _____

2. status indicator _____

3. ScreenTip _____

4. point _____

5. selected text _____

The Word Screen (5)

Identify the elements indicated in Figure WD1.

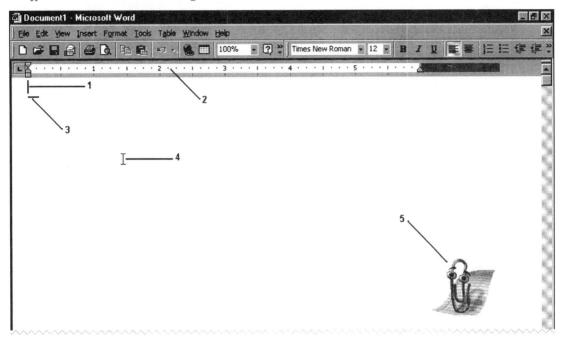

Figure WD1

1. _____   4. _____

2. _____   5. _____

3. _____

Multiple Choice (5)

Circle the letter of the best answer.

1. How are the four status indicators that display on the taskbar (REC, TRK, EXT, and OVR) turned on or off?
   a. click the status indicator
   b. right-click the status indicator
   c. double-click the status indicator
   d. drag the status indicator into the document window

2. How high is a character with a font size of 10 points?
   a. 10/12 of an inch
   b. 10/24 of an inch
   c. 10/36 of an inch
   d. 10/72 of an inch

3. What does a red wavy underline beneath a word mean?
   a. the word is misspelled
   b. the word is not in Word's dictionary
   c. the word contains a grammatical error
   d. Word can suggest a synonym

4. How can you scroll up one screen?
   a. click anywhere above the scroll box
   b. press CTRL+UP ARROW
   c. click the scroll arrow at the top of the scroll bar
   d. press CTRL+PAGE UP

5. What are the small squares called at each corner and the middle location of the selection rectangle that surrounds a selected graphic?
   a. sizing handles
   b. reset buttons
   c. location squares
   d. formatting tabs

Toolbar (5)

Identify and explain the purpose of each indicated toolbar button in Figure WD2.

Figure WD2

1. _____
2. _____
3. _____
4. _____
5. _____

Fill in the Blanks (5)

Write a word (or words) in the blank to complete each sentence correctly.

1. To display the entire Standard toolbar, double-click its _____, which is the vertical bar at the left edge of a toolbar.

2. Use the _____ command to increase or decrease the size of displayed characters to a point where the left and right margins are at the edges of the document window.

3. A(n) _____ is a specific location on a disk.

4. To change the font of characters in a headline, you must first _____, or highlight, the paragraphs in the headline.

5. The Office Assistant tip feature is part of the _____ that is built into Word, which understands what you are trying to do and suggests better ways to do it.

Sequence (5)

Use the numbers 1 – 5 to show the order in which these steps should be performed to save a new document on a floppy disk.

___   Click the Save in box arrow and then point to 3 ½ Floppy (A:).

___   In the Save As dialog box, type the file name in the File name text box.

___   Click the Save button in the Save As dialog box.

___   Click 3 ½ Floppy (A:) and then point to the Save button in the Save As dialog box.

___   Insert a formatted floppy disk into drive A. Click the Save button on the Standard toolbar.

Short Answer (5)

Write a brief answer to each question.

1. How is a floating toolbar different from a docked toolbar?

2. Why is it necessary to save a document that you will use later? How does saving a new document differ from saving an existing document?

3. When would you use the Format Picture dialog box to resize a graphic instead of dragging the sizing handles? Why?

4. When changes are made to a document, into what categories do the changes normally fall? When would each type of change be made?

5. How is overtype mode different from insert mode? How do you switch between overtype mode and insert mode?

Activities

Use Help

Use Help to answer each question.

1. How do you **change the color of text**? Use the Office Assistant to find out.

2. How can you **set the default font**? Using the Formatting book on the Contents sheet, look in the Formatting Characters book to find out.

3. How can you show a **tip of the day** when Word starts? Use the Index sheet to find out.

Expanding on the Lab

Perform the following tasks.

1. Open the Registration Announcement created in In the Lab 2.

2. Change the headline font to 24 point Brush Script MT.

3. Delete computer programming, in the announcement.

4. Change the cost from $75 to $100.

5. Change the font of *and much more* from italic to underlined. Change the font of variety from underlined to italic.

6. Insert the word personalized before payment plans.

7. Change Monday, August 27 to Wednesday, August 30.

8. Print the revised announcement.

9. Quit Word without saving the revised announcement.

Puzzle

The terms described by the phrases below are written below each line in code. Break the code by writing the correct term above the coded word. Then, use your broken code to translate the final sentences.

1. Full-featured word processing program that allows you to create professional looking documents.

   JFZOLPLCQ TLOA

2. Blinking vertical bar that indicates where text will be inserted as you type.

   FKPBOQFLK MLFKQ

3. Short horizontal line that indicates the termination of your document.

   BKA JXOH

4. Used to set tab stops, paragraph indents, column widths, and page margins.

   ORIBO

5. Used to display different portions of your document in the document window.

   PZOLII YXOP

6. Presents information about the location of the insertion point, progress of current tasks, and status of certain commands.

   PQXQRP YXO

7. Used to turn certain keys or modes on or off.

   PQXQRP FKAFZXQLOP

8. Displays the Word menu names.

   JBKR YXO

9. Contains buttons, boxes, and menus that allow you to perform tasks more quickly.

   QLLIYXO

10. Command used to increase or decrease the size of displayed characters so both the left and right margins appear in the document window.

    WLLJ MXDB TFAQE

11. Unit in which font size is measured.

    MLFKQ

12. Displays on the screen but is not visible in a printed document.

    CLOJXQQFKD JXOH

13. Allows you to type words in a paragraph without continually pressing the enter key at the end of each line.

    TLOATOXM

14. Indicates the current relative location of the insertion point in a document.

    PZOLII YLU

15. Default position of paragraphs.

    IBCQ-XIFDKBA

16. Can be used to cancel your most recent command(s) or action(s).

    RKAL YRQQLK

17. Series of predefined graphics included with Word 2000 that can be inserted into a Word document.

    ZIFM XOQ

18. Includes both enlarging and reducing the dimension of a graphic.

    OBPFWFKD

19. Printed version of a document.

_____

EXOA ZLMV

20. As you type, Word replaces the character to the left of the insertion point.

_____

LSBOQVMB JLAB

_____

QEB CLKQ QFJBP KBT OLJXK FP YXPBA LK IBQQBOP FKPZOFYBA FK QEB YXPB

_____

LC QOXGXK'P ZLIRJK FK QEB OLJXK CLORJ. QEFP BUMIXFKP QEB IFKBXO ZEXOXZQBO

_____

LC QEB IBQQBOP, PFKZB FQ FP AFCCFZRIQ QL ZEFPBI ZROSBP.

Microsoft Word 2000
Project Two
Creating a Research Paper

This project introduces creating a research paper with a table using the MLA documentation style. You learn how to change margin settings, adjust line spacing, create headers with page numbers, enter text using Click and Type, use shortcut keys to apply formatting, and indent paragraphs. You discover how to use the AutoCorrect feature. Then, you learn to add a footnote, modify a style, and automatically insert a symbol. You create an alphabetical works cited page, including inserting a manual page break, creating a hanging indent and hyperlink, and sorting paragraphs. You learn about proofing and revising a research paper by going to a specific location in a document, finding and replacing text, moving text, using word count, and checking spelling and grammar at once. Finally, you navigate to a hyperlink and e-mail a copy of the research paper.

Project Outline

I. Introduction [WD 2.4]

Many different styles of documentation exist for report preparation.

The MLA (Modern Language Association) and APA (American Psychological Association) are

_____

II. Project Two – Web Publishing Research Paper [WD 2.4]

   A. MLA documentation style [WD 2.6]

      Elements of MLA documentation style:

      • On each page _____

         _____

         _____

      • The title is _____

         _____

      • Parenthetical citations are _____

         _____

      • Explanatory notes are _____

         _____

      • Superscripts are used for _____

- Works cited are _____
  _____

B. Starting Word [WD 2.6]

  ☞ To start Word

    1. _____

    2. _____

    3. _____

    4. _____

C. Resetting menus and toolbars [WD 2.7]

  ☞ To reset menus and toolbars

    1. _____

    2. _____

       _____

    3. _____

    4. _____

D. Displaying formatting marks [WD 2.7]

  Formatting marks indicate _____

  ☞ To display formatting marks

    1. _____

       _____

III. Changing the margins [WD 2.7]

  Word is preset to use _____

  _____

  ☞ To change the default margin settings

    1. _____

    2. _____

    3. _____

       _____

    4. _____

A. Zooming page width [WD 2.9]

  When you zoom page width _____

  _____

  ☞ To zoom page width

    1. _____

    2. _____

IV.   Adjusting line spacing [WD 2.9]

Line spacing is _____

Although Word, by default, single-spaces between lines of text, the MLA style requires that you

double-space; that is, _____

☞ To double-space a document

1. _____

2. _____

_____

3. _____

4. _____

V.   Using a header to number pages [WD 2.11]

To place your name in front of the page number (as required by the MLA style), you must create a

header that contains the page number.

A.   Headers and footers [WD 2.11]

• A header is _____

• A footer is _____

☞ To display the header area

1. _____

2. _____

You can dock the floating Header and Footer toolbar by _____

_____

When you click the Header and Footer command, Word switches to print layout view, which

displays _____

B.   Entering text using Click and Type [WD 2.13]

In print layout view, Click and Type can be used to _____

_____

☞ To Click and Type

1. _____

As the Click and Type pointer is moved around the window _____

_____

2. _____

C.   Entering a page number into the header [WD 2.13]

☞ To enter and format a page number

1. _____

2. _____

_____

3. _____

To edit an existing header _____

To create a footer _____

_____

VI. Typing the body of the research paper [WD 2.15]

    A. Changing the default font size [WD 2.15]

        ☞ To change the default font size

        1. _____

        2. _____

    B. Entering name and course information [WD 2.15]

        ☞ To enter name and course information

        1. _____

_____

        An AutoComplete tip displays _____

_____

    C. Applying formatting using shortcut keys [WD 2.16]

    Shortcut keys sometimes can be used to format text as you type.

        ☞ To use shortcut keys to format text

        1. _____

        2. _____

    D. Saving the research paper [WD 2.18]

        ☞ To save a document

        1. _____

        2. _____

        3. _____

        4. _____

        5. _____

    E. Indenting paragraphs [WD 2.18]

    First-line indent is a procedure in which the first line of each paragraph is _____

_____

      • The First Line Indent marker is _____

      • The Left Indent marker is _____

☞ To first-line indent paragraphs

1. _____

2. _____

3. _____

4. _____

F. Using Word's AutoCorrect feature [WD 2.20]

AutoCorrect automatically _____

☞ To AutoCorrect as you type

1. _____

2. _____

You can add your own words to Word's predefined list of AutoCorrect entries.

☞ To create an AutoCorrect entry

1. _____

2. _____
_____

3. _____

To set an exception to an AutoCorrect rule _____

_____

_____

G. Adding footnotes [WD 2.23]

- A footnote displays _____

- An endnote displays _____

Note text can be _____

A note reference mark is located _____

If you rearrange, insert, or delete notes, Word automatically renumbers the notes.

☞ To add a footnote

1. _____

2. _____

3. _____

Word opens a note pane in the lower portion of the Word window with a note

reference mark positioned in the left margin.

4. _____

H. Modifying a style [WD 2.25]

A style is _____

The Normal style is _____

_____

☞   To modify a style

    1. _____

    2. _____

       _____

    3. _____

    4. _____

       _____

    5. _____

    6. _____

    7. _____

       _____

    8. _____

    9. _____

       _____

☞   To close the note pane

    1. _____

    2. _____

In normal view, the note text displays as a ScreenTip when you point to the note reference.

To delete a note _____

_____

To move a note _____

_____

To edit a note _____

_____

☞   To enter more text

    1. _____

    2. _____

I. Automatic page breaks [WD 2.31]

Automatic, or soft, page breaks are _____

_____

Background repagination is _____

In normal view, automatic page breaks appear on the screen as _____

☞   To page break automatically

    1. _____

       _____

By default, Word prevents widows and orphans from occurring in a document.

- A widow is _____

- An orphan occurs _____

J. Inserting arrows, faces, and other symbols automatically [WD 2.33]

The list of AutoCorrect entries also contains _____

☞ To insert a symbol automatically

     1. _____

         _____

     2. _____

     3. _____

         _____

VII. Creating an alphabetical works cited page [WD 2.34]

The works cited page is _____

_____

A. Manual page breaks [WD 2.34]

A manual, or hard, page break is _____

_____

Word never moves or adjusts manual page breaks.

☞ To page break manually

     1. _____

         _____

The manual page break displays _____

_____

To remove a manual page break _____

_____

B. Centering the title of the works cited page [WD 2.35]

☞ To center the title of the works cited page

     1. _____

     2. _____

     3. _____

     4. _____

     5. _____

C. Creating a hanging indent [WD 2.36]

A hanging indent is _____

_____

- The Hanging Indent marker is _____

☞ To create a hanging indent

    1. _____

    2. _____

☞ To enter work cited paragraphs

    1. _____

    2. _____

D. Creating a hyperlink [WD 2.38]

A hyperlink is _____

Jumping is _____

When you create a hyperlink to a Web page, you do not need to be connected to the Internet.

☞ To create a hyperlink as you type

    1. _____

    2. _____

E. Sorting paragraphs [WD 2.39]

Sorting is _____

You can arrange paragraphs in _____

☞ To sort paragraphs

    1. _____

    _____

    2. _____

    3. _____

You can undo a sort by _____

By default, Word sorts in ascending sort order.

- Ascending sort order means _____

- Descending sort order means _____

VIII. Proofing and revising the research paper [WD 2.41]

While proofreading, you _____

A. Going to a specific location in a document [WD 2.41]

The Select Browse Object menu provides _____

☞ To browse by page

    1. _____

    _____

    2. _____

    3. _____

B. Finding and replacing text [WD 2.43]

    ☞ To find and replace text

        1. _____

        _____

        2. _____

        _____

        3. _____

        4. _____

    To instruct Word to confirm each change _____

    _____

C. Finding text [WD 2.45]

    ☞ To find text

        1. _____

        _____

        2. _____

        _____

D. Moving text [WD 2.45]

    To move text, you first select the text to be moved and then use drag-and-drop editing or the cut-and-paste technique.

    • With drag-and-drop editing, you _____

    _____

    • Cutting involves _____

    • Pasting is _____

    ☞ To select a sentence

        1. _____

        _____

    ☞ To move text

        1. _____

        When you begin to drag text, the insertion point changes to a dotted insertion point.

        2. _____

        3. _____

    If you hold the CTRL key down while dragging, Word _____

E. Finding a synonym [WD 2.48]

    Synonyms are _____

    A thesaurus is _____

    ☞ To find a synonym

      1. _____

         _____

      2. _____

F. Using Word Count [WD 2.48]

Word Count displays the number of words, pages, characters, paragraphs, and lines in a document.

    ☞ To count words

      1. _____

      2. _____

      3. _____

G. Checking spelling and grammar at once [WD 2.50]

    ☞ To check spelling and grammar at once

      1. _____

         _____

      2. _____

         _____

      3. _____

      4. _____

      5. _____

         _____

H. Saving again and printing the document [WD 2.52]

    ☞ To save a document again

      1. _____

    ☞ To print a document

      1. _____

IX. Navigating a hyperlink [WD 2.53]

    ☞ To navigate a hyperlink

      1. _____

      2. _____

      3. _____

         _____

X. E-mailing a copy of the research paper [WD 2.54]

☞ To e-mail a document

1. _____

_____

☞ To quit Word

1. _____

Review

Matching (5)

Match each formatting task on the left with the appropriate shortcut keys from the right.

____ 1. all capital letters

____ 2. double-underline

____ 3. superscript

____ 4. decrease paragraph indent

____ 5. remove hanging indent

a. CTRL+SHIFT+PLUS SIGN

b. CTRL+SHIFT+K

c. CTRL+SHIFT+T

d. CTRL+SHIFT+A

e. CTRL+SHIFT+M

f. CTRL+SHIFT+D

g. CTRL+SHIFT+W

True/False (10)

*Circle **T** if the statement is true and **F** if the statement is false.*

T F   1. An endnote displays at the bottom of the page on which its reference mark appears.

T F   2. Explanatory notes are used to elaborate on points discussed in a research paper.

T F   3. MLA documentation style requires that the entire document be double-spaced, except for the works cited page.

T F   4. Headers display in the document window in normal view.

T F   5. You can center a paragraph before typing it.

T F   6. Word's page width zoom brings both the left and right margins into view in the document window.

T F   7. Explanatory notes are mandatory in the MLA documentation style.

T F   8. An orphan is created when the first line of a paragraph displays by itself at the bottom of a page.

T F   9. By default, Word orders in ascending sort order, which means from the beginning of the alphabet to the end, from the smallest number to the largest, or from the earliest date to the most recent.

T F   10. The Word Count command appears on the Tools menu.

Definitions (5)

Briefly define each term.

1. line spacing _____

2. AutoComplete tip _____

3. style _____

4. background repagination _____

5. hanging indent _____

The Word Screen (5)

Identify the Header and Footer toolbar buttons indicated in Figure WD3.

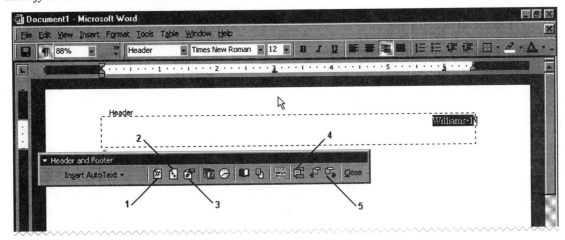

Figure WD3

1. _____   4. _____

2. _____   5. _____

3. _____

Multiple Choice (5)

Circle the letter of the best answer.

1. Which is *not* an MLA documentation style requirement?
   a. double-spaced text
   b. separate title page
   c. works cited page
   d. page numbers

2. What are Word's default margins?
   a. 1-inch top, bottom, left, and right
   b. 1.25-inch top, bottom, left, and right
   c. 1-inch left and right, and 1.25-inch top and bottom
   d. 1.25-inch left and right, and 1-inch top and bottom

3. Which keys do you press to center a paragraph before typing?
   a. CTRL+E
   b. CTRL+C
   c. CTRL+L
   d. CTRL+O

4. How would you first-line indent the paragraphs in a research paper one-half inch?
   a. drag the top triangle at the 0" mark on the ruler to the .5" mark
   b. drag the bottom triangle at the 0" mark on the ruler to the .5" mark
   c. drag the triangle at the 6.5" mark on the ruler to the 6" mark
   d. drag the small square at the 0" mark on the ruler to the .5" mark

5. How do you delete a note?
   a. select the note reference mark in the note pane (not in the document window) and then click the Cut button on the Standard toolbar
   b. click to the left of the note reference mark in the document window and then press the BACKSPACE key twice
   c. select the note reference mark in the document window (not in the note pane) and then click the Cut button on the Standard toolbar
   d. click to the right of the note reference mark in the document window and then press the DELETE key twice

Dialog Box (5)

Answer the following questions about the AutoCorrect dialog box shown in Figure WD4.

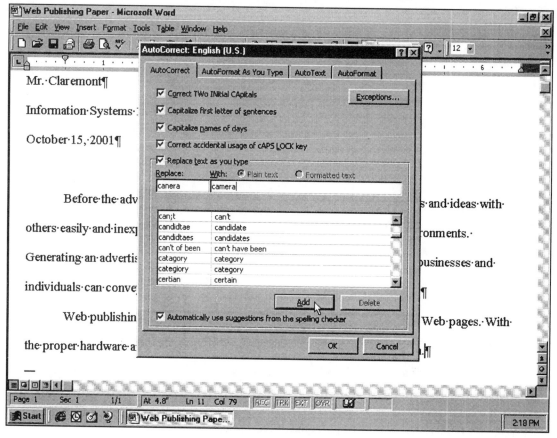

Figure WD4

1. How would you display this dialog box? _____

2. What misspelled word is being added? _____

3. Between what two words will the new entry be placed? _____

4. What would you click to include the new word in the list of AutoCorrect entries? _____

5. How would you exit the dialog box without adding the new word? _____

Fill in the Blanks (5)

Write a word (or words) in the blank to complete each sentence correctly.

1. The MLA style uses in-text _____ instead of footnoting each source at the bottom of the page.

2. It is helpful to display _____ that indicate where in the document you pressed the ENTER key, SPACEBAR, and other keys.

3. Word automatically numbers notes sequentially by placing a(n) _____ in the body of the document and also in front of the note text.

4. The base style for new Word documents is called the _____, which for a new installation of Word 2000 more likely uses 12-point Times New Roman font for characters.

5. _____ is the process of following a hyperlink to its destination.

Sequence (5)

Use the numbers 1 – 5 to show the order in which these steps should be performed to double-space a new document.

___ Click Paragraph on the shortcut menu. If necessary, click the Indents and Spacing tab.

___ Click the OK button.

___ Right-click the paragraph mark above the end mark in the document window.

___ Click the Line spacing box arrow.

___ Click Double.

Short Answer (5)

Write a brief answer to each question.

1. In the Line spacing list, how are the At least option, Exactly option, and Multiple option different? Which option is best if a document contains larger fonts and graphics? Why?

2. Why is setting a first-line indent more efficient than simply using the TAB key to indent the first line of a paragraph? For what purpose is the Left Indent marker used?

3. What kind of capitalization errors can the AutoCorrect feature correct? How can you turn off the AutoCorrect feature?

4. How is a widow different from an orphan? What would you do if you wanted to allow widows and orphans?

5. How is a manual page break (hard page break) different from an automatic page break (soft page break)? When does each occur?

Activities

Use Help

Use Help to answer each question.

1. How do you **sort according to the rules of another language**? Use the Office Assistant to find out.

2. How do you convert **footnotes** to endnotes and vice versa? Use the Index sheet to find out.

3. How can you **find and replace paragraph marks, page breaks, and other items**? Using the Editing and Sorting Text book on the Contents sheet, look in the Finding and Replacing Text and Formatting book to find out.

Expanding on the Lab

Perform the following tasks.

1. Open the file named Virtual Reality Paper that you created in In the Lab 2.

2. Add a footnote to the second sentence of the first paragraph of the report, to read as follows: Brown estimates that nearly 95% of VR applications take this form.

3. Use the thesaurus to replace the word, requires, in the first sentence of the first paragraph with an appropriate synonym.

4. Add an entry to the end of the works cited page, as follows: Grant, William. *A Brief History of Virtual Reality*. Chicago: Scientific Press, Inc., 2000.

5. Sort the works cited in ascending order.

6. Print the revised paper.

7. Quit Word without saving the revised paper.

Puzzle

Write the word described by each clue in the puzzle below. Words can be written forward or backward, across, up and down, or diagonally. The first letter of each word already appears in the puzzle.

Popular documentation style for research paper.

Used for note reference marks.

Type of notes used to elaborate on points discussed in the paper.

MLA term for bibliographical references.

Type of marks that indicate where ENTER and other nonprinting keys were pressed.

Attach a floating toolbar.

Can be used in print layout view to format and enter text.

Marker used to change the entire left margin.

Explanatory note at the bottom of a page.

Explanatory note at the end of a document.

In Word, can be any length and format.

Customized format that can be applied to text.

Displays note text when you point to a note reference mark.

Type of page break inserted automatically.

Created when the last line of a paragraph displays by itself at the top of a page.

Occurs when the first line of a paragraph displays by itself at the bottom of a page.

Type of page break forced into a document at a specific location.

Shortcut that allows users to jump to another location.

Words similar in meaning.

Book of synonyms.

Tools menu command that ascertains the number of words in a document.

Microsoft Word 2000

Project Three
Using a Wizard to Create a Resume and Creating a Cover Letter with a Table

~~~~~~

Overview

This project introduces creating a resume using Word's Resume Wizard. Several formatting techniques are used to personalize the resume. You view and print the resume in print preview. You learn how to add color to characters, set and use tab stops, collect and paste, insert a symbol and add a bottom border to a paragraph. You learn to identify the components of a business letter, as you create and personalize the cover letter. An AutoText entry is created and inserted. You also learn how to insert a nonbreaking space, create a bulleted list as you type, enter data into a Word table, and format a Word table. Finally, you prepare and print an envelope address and close multiple Word documents.

Project Outline

   I. Introduction [WD 3.4]

      A resume contains _____

      You should design your resume carefully so that it presents you as the best candidate for the job.

      A cover letter enables you to _____

      Word provides wizards and templates to assist you in document preparation.

      • A template is _____

      • Word's wizards prepare and format a document based on _____

         _____

  II. Project Three – Resume and Cover Letter [WD 3.4]

 III. Using Word's Resume Wizard to create a resume [WD 3.6]

      You can create a resume from scratch or you can use Word's Resume Wizard and _____

      _____

      A wizard's dialog box displays a list of panel names along _____

      _____

      ☞ To create a resume using Word's Resume Wizard

        1. _____

          _____

2. _____

    The Start panel informs _____

    You can click a Microsoft Word Help button to _____

3. _____

_____

    The Style panel requests _____

4. _____

_____

    The Type panel asks _____

5. _____

    The Address panel displays _____

6. _____

_____

_____

_____

7. _____

_____

    The Standard Headings panel requests _____

8. _____

    The Optional Headings panel allows _____

9. _____

    The Add/Sort Heading panel allows _____

10. _____

_____

11. _____

12. _____

_____

_____

13. _____

14. _____

_____

_____

When using the Resume Wizard

- Click the Back button to _____
- Click the Cancel button to _____

In addition to the Resume Wizard, Word provides wizards to assist in creating _____

_____

Word displays the resume in print layout view.

Print layout view shows _____

In print layout view

- The Print Layout View button displays _____

- A vertical ruler displays _____

A. Resetting menus and toolbars [WD 3.13]

   ☞ To reset menus and toolbars

      1. _____

      2. _____

      3. _____

      4. _____

   ☞ To print the resume created by the Resume Wizard

      1. _____

      2. _____

IV. Personalizing the resume [WD 3.15]

   A. Displaying formatting marks [WD 3.15]

      Formatting marks indicate _____

      ☞ To display formatting marks

         1. _____

   B. Tables [WD 3.15]

      A Word table is _____

      - A cell is _____

         The end-of-cell mark is _____

      - Gridlines help _____

         Click Show Gridlines on the Table menu to _____

         Click Hide Gridlines on the Table menu to _____

      - The table move handle allows you to _____

   C. Zooming text width [WD 3.16]

      Zoom text width to _____

      ☞ To zoom text width

         1. _____

         2. _____

☞ To bold text

1. _____

2. _____

D. Styles [WD 3.17]

A style is _____

Paragraph styles affect an entire paragraph; character styles affect only selected characters.

- In the Style list, paragraph style names are _____

- In the Style list, character style names are _____

E. Selecting and replacing text [WD 3.18]

Placeholder text is _____

☞ To select and replace placeholder text

1. _____

2. _____

☞ To select and replace Resume Wizard supplied text

1. _____
   _____

2. _____
   _____

3. _____
   _____

A bullet is _____

A bulleted list is _____

☞ To enter placeholder text

1. _____

2. _____

3. _____

4. _____

5. _____

F. Entering a line break [WD 3.21]

A line break advances _____
_____

☞ To enter a line break

1. _____
   _____

   A line break character is _____

2. _____

☞   To enter the remaining sections of the resume

1. _____

2. _____

3. _____

4. _____

5. _____

6. _____

7. _____

8. _____

V.   Viewing and printing the resume in print preview [WD 3.24]

Print preview displays _____

The Shrink to Fit button allows you to _____

☞   To print preview a document

1. _____
   _____

2. _____

   The Print Preview toolbar displays _____

3. _____
   _____

   Word displays a grid so _____

4. _____
   _____

5. _____

6. _____
   _____

7. _____

A.   Saving the resume [WD 3.26]

☞   To save a document

1. _____

2. _____

3. _____

4. _____

5. _____

VI. Creating a letterhead [WD 3.27]

For personal letters, creating a letterhead and saving it in a file is an inexpensive alternative to purchasing stationery with preprinted letterhead.

A. Opening a new document window [WD 3.27]

☞ To open a new document window

1. _____

2. _____

☞ To change the font size

1. _____

2. _____

B. Adding color to characters [WD 3.28]

☞ To color characters

1. _____

2. _____

The color palette displays _____

3. _____

☞ To enter and resize a graphic

1. _____

2. _____

3. _____

4. _____

5. _____

C. Setting tab stops using the Tabs dialog box [WD 3.30]

By default, Word places tab stops _____

• Small tick marks indicate _____

When you set a custom tab stop, Word _____

At a tab stop, text can be aligned _____

Word stores tab settings _____

☞ To set custom tab stops using the Tab dialog box

1. _____

_____

2. _____

_____

3. _____

A tab marker is _____

A tab character displays _____

D. Collecting and pasting [WD 3.32]

The Office Clipboard is used to collect _____

Pasting is _____

☞ To switch from one open document to another

1. _____

2. _____

☞ To collect items

1. _____

_____

2. _____

_____

_____

_____

3. _____

4. _____

_____

_____

The Office Clipboard can store _____

☞ To paste from the Office Clipboard

1. _____

2. _____

3. _____

4. _____

_____

5. _____

Click the Paste All button on the Clipboard toolbar to _____

Click the Clear Clipboard button on the Clipboard toolbar to _____

☞ To color more characters the same color

1. _____

_____

2. _____

E. Inserting symbols into a document [WD 3.37]

☞ To insert a symbol into text

1. _____

_____

2. _____

_____

3. _____

_____

4. _____

ANSI characters are _____

F. Adding a bottom border to a paragraph [WD 3.39]

A border is _____

☞ To add a bottom border to a paragraph

1. _____

_____

_____

2. _____

The border palette is used to _____

3. _____

To remove a border _____

☞ To change the color of text

1. _____

2. _____

☞ To save the letterhead

1. _____

2. _____

3. _____

4. _____

5. _____

VII. Creating a cover letter [WD 3.41]

A. Components of a business letter [WD 3.41]

A cover letter is _____

Essential business letter elements:

- date line _____

- inside address _____

- salutation _____

- message _____

- complimentary close _____

- signature block _____

In the modified block style _____

_____

B. Saving the cover letter with a new file name [WD 3.42]

☞ To save the document with a new file name

     1. _____

     2. _____

     3. _____

     4. _____

     5. _____

☞ To increase the font size

     1. _____

     2. _____

C. Setting tab stops using the ruler [WD 3.42]

☞ To set custom tab stops using the ruler

     1. _____

          _____

     2. _____

To move a custom tab stop _____

To remove a custom tab stop _____

☞ To enter the date, inside address, and salutation

     1. _____

     2. _____

     3. _____

D. Creating an AutoText entry [WD 3.44]

An AutoText entry stores _____

☞ To create an AutoText entry

     1. _____

          _____

     2. _____

          _____

     3. _____

E. Entering a nonbreaking space [WD 3.46]

A nonbreaking space is _____

_____

A nonbreaking hyphen is _____

_____

☞ To insert a nonbreaking space

    1. _____

    _____

    2. _____

F. Inserting an AutoText entry [WD 3.47]

  ☞ To insert an AutoText entry

    1. _____

    2. _____

An AutoComplete tip is _____

☞ To enter a paragraph

    1. _____

    2. _____

    3. _____

G. AutoFormat as you type [WD 3.49]

Word can apply some formats automatically as you type.

☞ To bullet a list as you type

    1. _____

    2. _____

    3. _____

    4. _____

To stop bulleting paragraphs _____

To number a list automatically _____

_____

☞ To enter a paragraph

    1. _____

    2. _____

H. Creating a table with the Insert Table button [WD 3.52]

The dimension of a table is _____

☞ To insert an empty table

    1. _____

    _____

    _____

    2. _____

I. Inserting data into a Word table [WD 3.53]

To advance rightward from one cell to the next _____

To add new rows to a table _____

☞   To enter data into a table

    1. _____

    2. _____

To delete the contents of a cell _____

J.   Formatting a table [WD 3.55]

  ☞   To AutoFormat a table

    1. _____

    2. _____

       _____

    3. _____

K.   Changing the table alignment [WD 3.56]

  ☞   To select a table

    1. _____

       _____

    2. _____

    3. _____

       _____

  ☞   To enter the remainder of the cover letter

    1. _____

    2. _____

    3. _____

    4. _____

L.   Saving again and printing the cover letter [WD 3.58]

  ☞   To save a document again

    1. _____

  ☞   To print a document

    1. _____

VIII.   Preparing and printing an envelope address [WD 3.58]

  ☞   To prepare and print an envelope address

    1. _____

       _____

    2. _____

       _____

    3. _____

☞ To close all open Word documents

    1. _____

    2. _____

☞ To quit Word

    1. _____

Review

Matching (5)

Match each term on the left with the best description from the right.

___	1. table	a.	drag to move a table to a new location
___	2. cell	b.	intersection of a row and a column
___	3. end-of-cell mark	c.	collection of rows and columns
___	4. gridlines	d.	similar to a form with prewritten text
___	5. table move handle	e.	nonprinting character used to select and format cells
		f.	help identify rows and columns
		g.	temporary Windows storage area

True/False (10)

*Circle **T** if the statement is true and **F** if the statement is false.*

T   F   1.   The Optional Headings panel in the Resume Wizard dialog box allows you to type any additional headings you want on your resume.

T   F   2.   When Word displays a resume generated by the Resume Wizard in the document window, it switches from page layout view to normal view.

T   F   3.   In normal view, the Print Layout View button on the horizontal scroll bar is recessed.

T   F   4.   Unlike normal view, print layout view shows you exactly how the printed page will look.

T   F   5.   Selected placeholder text is deleted automatically as soon as you begin typing.

T   F   6.   Press CTRL+ENTER to insert a line break.

T   F   7.   If a document *spills* onto a second page, you can try to shrink the document so it fits onto a single page using the Shrink to Fit button in print preview.

T   F   8.   When you set a custom tab stop, Word clears all default tab stops to the right of the custom tab stop.

T   F   9.   When you copy a thirteenth item to the Office Clipboard, Word deletes the last item to make room for the new item.

T   F   10. When you are in the rightmost cell in a row, press the ENTER key to move to the first cell in the next row of the table.

Definitions (5)

Briefly define each term.

1.   placeholder text _____

2.   bullet _____

3.   line break _____

4.   tab character _____

5.   nonbreaking space _____

The Word Screen (5)

Identify the indicated buttons on the Print Preview toolbar in Figure WD5.

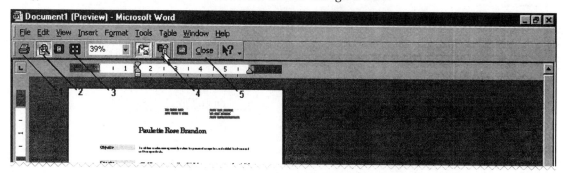

Figure WD5

1. _____   4. _____

2. _____   5. _____

3. _____

Multiple Choice (5)

Circle the letter of the best answer.

1. Which buttons in the Add/Sort heading panel are clicked to rearrange resume headings in a resume being generated with the Resume Wizard?
    a. Add or Remove
    b. Back or Next
    c. Move Up or Move Down
    d. Cancel or Finish

2. Which of the following happens in page layout view?
    a. the Page Layout View button is recessed
    b. a vertical ruler displays at the left edge of the document window
    c. the entire piece of paper is positioned in the document window
    d. all of the above

3. What would you click on the Table menu to better identify the rows and columns in a table?
    a. Split Table
    b. Table Properties
    c. Show Gridlines
    d. Draw Table

4. By default, where does Word place tab stops on the ruler?
    a. at every .125" mark
    b. at every .25" mark
    c. at every .5" mark
    d. at every 1" mark

5. What do you press to enter a special type of hyphen that prevents two words separated by a hyphen from splitting at the end of a line?
    a. CTRL+SHIFT+HYPHEN
    b. ALT+CTRL+HYPHEN
    c. SHIFT+ALT+HYPHEN
    d. TAB+ALT+HYPHEN

Dialog Box (5)

Answer the following questions about the Resume Wizard dialog box shown in Figure WD6.

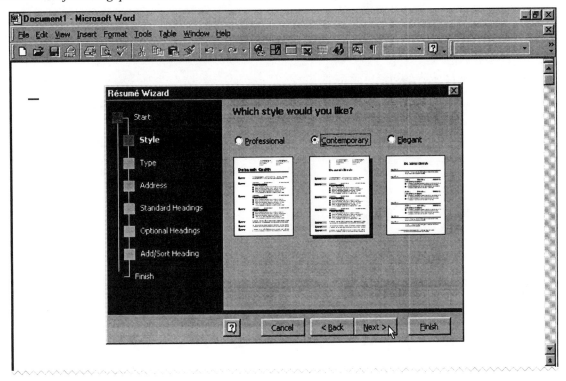

Figure WD6

1. How was the dialog box displayed? _____

2. Which resume style is selected? _____

3. How would you advance to the next panel? _____

4. What panel will display next? _____

5. What button would you click to change options in previous panels? _____

Fill in the Blanks (5)

Write a word (or words) in the blank to complete each sentence correctly.

1. _____ displays an entire document in reduced size on the Word screen so you can see exactly how it will look when printed.

2. Default tab marks are indicated on the horizontal ruler by small _____.

3. In Word you can draw a solid line, called a(n) _____, at any edge of a paragraph.

4. In the _____ letter, the date, complimentary close, and signature block are centered, and all other letter components begin flush with the left margin.

5. The _____ of a table is the total number of rows and columns.

Sequence (5)

Use the numbers 1 – 5 to show the order in which these steps should be performed to create an AutoText entry.

_____   Type the name of the AutoText entry.

_____   Drag through the text to be stored.

_____   Click New on the AutoText submenu.

_____   Click the OK button.

_____   Click Insert on the menu bar, then point to AutoText.

Short Answer (5)

Write a brief answer to each question.

1. How is a template different from a wizard?

2. What is the difference between a paragraph style and a character style? How are the style names differentiated in the Style list?

3. What are the components of a business letter? Which, if any, are optional?

4. When would it be useful to create an AutoText entry? How is an AutoText entry different from an AutoCorrect entry?

5. What is an AutoComplete tip? For what items does Word propose them? How do you ignore the AutoComplete tip?

Activities

Use Help

Use Help to answer each question.

1. How do you turn the **AutoFormat As You Type** feature on and off? Use the Office Assistant to find out.

2. How do you edit an **AutoText** entry? Use the Index sheet to find out.

3. How do you **skip text during a spelling and grammar check**? Use the Checking Spelling and Grammar book on the Contents sheet to find out.

Expanding on the Lab

Perform the following tasks.

1. Open the file named Schumann Resume that you created in In the Lab 1.

2. Select the entire table (the resume itself) and change the font to Times New Roman 12 (or a similar font).

3. Draw a border under the name, David Paul Schumann.

4. Use drag-and-drop editing techniques to switch Alpha Beta Lambda Fraternity, Vice President with Nutrition Services of America in the Memberships section.

5. Move the Work Experience section so that it is placed above the Languages section. Change Serve dining patrons to Function as maitre d'.

6. Add Painting to the list of Hobbies.

7. Italicize each heading in the left column (i.e., Objective, Education, Awards received, and so on).

8. View the revised resume from within print preview. If the resume exceeds one page, use print preview to shrink it to a page. Print the revised resume.

9. Quit Word without saving the revised resume.

Puzzle

All of the words described below appear in the puzzle. Words may be either forward or backward, across, up and down, or diagonal. Circle each word as you find it.

Using a Wizard

```
T  ■  ■  T  ■  N  O  I  T  A  T  U  L  A  S
X  S  S  E  R  D  D  A  E  D  I  S  N  I  E
E  K  A  M  S  R  C  B  L  V  E  ■  G  P  N
T  R  U  P  P  E  O  O  L  E  G  N  ■  R  I
R  A  T  L  O  S  V  R  U  R  A  O  G  I  L
E  M  O  A  T  U  E  D  B  T  S  I  N  N  D
D  K  T  T  S  M  R  E  U  I  S  S  I  T  I
L  C  E  E  B  E  L  R  J  C  E  N  T  P  R
O  I  X  P  A  N  E  L  N  A  M  E  S  R  G
H  T  T  ■  T  B  T  A  B  L  E  M  A  E  W
E  E  N  I  L  E  T  A  D  R  ■  I  P  V  I
C  ■  C  O  L  L  E  C  T  U  ■  D  ■  I  Z
A  ■  C  O  L  O  R  P  A  L  E  T  T  E  A
L  K  ■  L  I  N  E  B  R  E  A  K  ■  W  R
P  ■  ■  G  N  I  K  A  E  R  B  N  O  N  D
```

Usually contains a job applicant's educational background and work experience.

Elaborates on the positive points in a resume.

Similar to a form with prewritten text.

Prepares and formats a document based on responses to several basic questions.

Listed on the left side of the Resume Wizard dialog box.

In print layout view, displays at the left edge of the document window.

A collection of rows and columns.

The intersection of a row and a column.

Help identify the rows and columns in a table.

Text in the Resume wizard resume that is replaced with personal information.

Symbol positioned at the beginning of a paragraph.

Advances the insertion point to the beginning of the next line, ignoring paragraph formatting instructions.

Displays the entire document in reduced size on the Word screen.

Displays when the Multiple Pages button on the Print Preview toolbar is clicked.

Displays when the Font Color button arrow is clicked.

Set, by default, at every .5" mark on the ruler.

Indicated default tabs on the horizontal ruler.

Copy multiple items to the Office Clipboard.

Process of copying an item from the Office Clipboard into a document.

Solid line that can be drawn at any edge of a paragraph.

In a letter, consists of the month, day, and year.

In a letter, placed three to eight lines below the date line.

If present in a letter, begins two lines below the last line of the inside address.

The body of a letter.

Typed at least four lines below a letter's complimentary close, allowing room for the author's name.

Entry stored and used throughout a document.

Type of space that prevents two words from splitting if the first word falls at the end of a line.

The specified number of rows and columns in a table.

Key used to advance rightward from one cell in a table to the next.

Microsoft Word 2000

Web Feature
Creating Web Pages Using Word

~~~~~~

Overview

This Web Feature introduces creating a Web page by saving an existing Word document and creating a Web page by using the Web Page Wizard. On the personal Web page, you create a hyperlink to the resume Web page and a hyperlink to your e-mail program.

Project Outline

I. Introduction [WDW 1.1]

Word provides two techniques for creating Web pages:

- _____

- _____

Word's Web page authoring features include _____

_____

A frame is _____

The frames page is _____

Publishing is _____

II. Saving a Word document as a Web page [WDW 1.3]

☞ To save a Word document as a Web page

1. _____

_____

2. _____

_____

3. _____

Word switches to _____

The document displays on the screen similar to _____

A. Formatting the e-mail address as a hyperlink [WDW 1.4]

☞ To format a hyperlink automatically

1. _____

2. _____

☞   To save and close a Web page

1. _____

2. _____

III.   Using Word's Web Page Wizard to create a Web page   [WDW 1.4]

The Web Page Wizard is used to _____

☞   To create a Web page using the Web Page Wizard

1. _____
_____

2. _____
_____
_____

The Title and Location panel displays _____

3. _____

The Navigation panel displays _____

4. _____

The Add Pages panel displays _____

5. _____
_____

6. _____

7. _____
_____

The Organize Pages panel allows _____

8. _____

9. _____
_____

The Visual Theme panel displays _____

A theme is _____

10. _____
_____

When creating a Web page using the Web Page Wizard, at any time you can click:

•   The Back button to _____

•   The Microsoft Word Help button to _____

•   The Cancel button to _____

IV.   Modifying a Web page   [WDW 1.8]

A frame border separates _____

☞ To resize a Web page frame

    1. _____

    2. _____

☞ To enter and format text

    1. _____

    2. _____

    3. _____

☞ To add a hyperlink

    1. _____

    _____

    _____

    2. _____

To edit an existing hyperlink _____

_____

☞ To save the frames page with a new file name

    1. _____

    2. _____

    3. _____

    4. _____

    5. _____

A. Viewing the Web page in your default browser [WDW 1.11]

    Use the Web Page Preview command to _____

    ☞ To quit Word

        1. _____

B. Editing a Web page from your browser [WDW 1.11]

    ☞ To edit a Web page from your browser

        1. _____

        _____

        _____

        2. _____

        3. _____

        4. _____

        5. _____

        6. _____

Review

Matching (3)

Match each term on the left with the best description from the right.

___ 1. Navigation panel
___ 2. Organize panel
___ 3. Theme panel

a. used to specify the sequence and names of hyperlinks

b. used to choose the placement of hyperlinks on a Web page

c. used to add pages to and remove pages from a Web site

d. used to enter the title and location of a Web site

e. used to select a collection of design elements and color schemes

True/False (5)

*Circle **T** if the statement is true and **F** if the statement is false.*

T   F   1. A hyperlink is a shortcut that allows users to jump easily and quickly to another location in the same document or to other documents or Web pages.

T   F   2. When you press the TAB or SHIFT key after a Web or e-mail address, Word automatically formats it as a hyperlink.

T   F   3. When creating a Web page using the Web Page Wizard, you can click the Next button in any panel to change any previously entered information.

T   F   4. When you point to a frame border, the mouse pointer changes to a double-headed arrow.

T   F   5. If you click File on the menu bar and then click Web Page Preview, Word opens your Web browser in a separate window and displays the open Web page in the browser window.

Fill in the Blanks (3)

Write a word (or words) in the blank to correctly complete each sentence.

1. A(n) _____ is a rectangular section of a Web page that can display multiple Web pages simultaneously.

2. _____ is the process of making Web pages available to others, for example, on the World Wide Web or on a company's intranet.

3. You can use the _____ or a Web page template to create a Web page from scratch.

Multiple Choice (2)

Circle the letter of the best answer.

1. What menu has the command you can use to save a Word document as a Web page?
    a. File
    b. Format
    c. Tools
    d. View

2. What is the first panel in the Web Page Wizard dialog box?
   a. the Navigation panel
   b. the Organize Pages panel
   c. the Visual Theme panel
   d. the Title and Location panel

Dialog Box (5)

Answer the following questions about the Insert Hyperlink dialog box shown in Figure WD7.

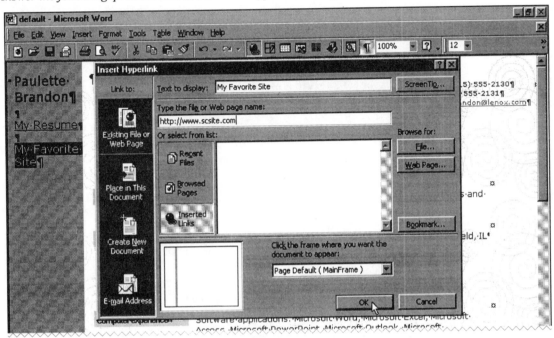

Figure WD7

1. How was the dialog box displayed? _____

2. What text is being formatted as a hyperlink? _____

3. To what is the hyperlink linked? _____

4. What is the Web address of the link? _____

5. How do you finish adding the hyperlink? _____

Short Answer (2)

Write a brief answer to each question.

1. How is creating a new Web page different from converting an existing Word document to a Web page?

2. Why is the Web Page Preview command a valuable aid when creating Web pages?

Activities

Use Help

Use Help to answer each question.

1. How do you **open a Web search page** from Word? Use the Office Assistant to find out.

2. How can **you change the display of a text in a hyperlink**? Use the Index sheet to find out.

Expanding on the Lab

Perform the following tasks.

1. Open the file containing your personal Web page that you created in In the Lab 3.

2. Remove at least three URLs that you inserted in the bullet list.

3. Enter at least five new URLs in the bullet list. If your list contained fewer than three items in the bullet list, insert URLs until you have at least five.

4. Test your Web page links, then save the revised document with Revised Personal Web Page as the file name.

Microsoft Excel 2000

Project One
Creating a Worksheet and Embedded Chart

Overview

In creating the worksheet and chart in this project, you gain a broad knowledge about Excel. First, you are introduced to starting Excel. You learn about the Excel window and how to enter text and numbers to create a worksheet. Selecting a range and using the AutoSum button to sum the numbers in a row or column are explained. You find out how to copy a cell to adjacent cells using the fill handle. Once the worksheet is built, you change the font size of the title, bold the title, and center the title across a range using buttons on the Formatting toolbar. Steps and techniques are presented to format the body of the worksheet using the AutoFormat command. You use the Chart Wizard to add a 3-D Column chart. After completing the worksheet, you save the workbook on disk and print the worksheet and chart. Editing data in cells is explained. Finally, you discover how to use the Excel Help system to answer your questions.

Project Outline

  I. What is Microsoft Excel 2000? [E 1.6]

     Microsoft Excel is _____

     _____

     Major parts of Excel:

- Worksheets allow _____
- Charts pictorially represent _____
- Databases manage _____
- Web support allows _____

  II. Project One – Fun-N-Sun Sojourn First Quarter Sales [E 1.6]

    A. Starting Excel [E 1.8]

      ☞ To start Excel

        1. _____

        2. _____

        3. _____

        4. _____

  III. The Excel worksheet [E 1.9]

     A workbook is _____

Worksheets are _____

A sheet tab displays _____

A. The worksheet [E 1.9]

    A worksheet is organized into a rectangular grid containing columns and rows.

    The column heading is _____

    The row heading is _____

    A cell is _____

    Each worksheet has 256 columns and 65,536 rows, or 16,777,216 cells.

    A cell reference is _____

    To identify a cell, specify _____

    The active cell is _____

    Ways to identify the active cell:

    • _____

    • _____

    • _____

    Gridlines are _____

    The mouse pointer displays as:

    • a block plus sign whenever _____

    • the block arrow whenever _____

IV. Worksheet window [E 1.11]

    A worksheet window is _____

    Scroll bars, scroll arrows, and scroll boxes can be used to _____

    The tab split box is _____

A. Menu bar [E 1.12]

    The worksheet menu bar displays _____

    Each menu name represents _____

    To display a menu _____

    • A short menu displays _____

    • A full menu lists _____

    Techniques used to display a full menu:

    1. _____

    2. _____

    3. _____

    4. _____

On a full menu:

- A hidden command displays _____

- A dimmed command displays _____

B. Standard toolbar and Formatting toolbar [E 1.12]

The Standard toolbar and Formatting toolbar contain _____

_____

A ScreenTip displays _____

To display the entire Standard or Formatting toolbar _____

The More Buttons button can be used to _____

C. Resetting menus and toolbars [E 1.14]

☞ To reset my usage data and toolbar buttons [MO C.1]

1. _____

2. _____

_____

3. _____

_____

4. _____

_____

5. _____

D. Formula bar [E 1.14]

The formula bar displays _____

The Name box displays _____

E. Status bar [E 1.14]

The status bar displays _____

_____

Mode indicators display _____

- Ready means _____

- Enter means _____

The AutoCalculate area can be used _____

Keyboard indicators show _____

V. Selecting a cell [E 1.15]

To enter data into a cell, you first must select it.

To select a cell, either

- Use the mouse to _____

- Use the arrow keys that _____

VI. Entering text [E 1.15]

In Excel, text is _____

A. Entering the worksheet title [E 1.16]

   ☞ To enter the worksheet title

     1. _____

     2. _____

        The insertion point is _____

     3. _____

     4. _____

Clicking the Enter box or pressing the ENTER key _____

Clicking the Cancel box _____

Text is left-aligned, meaning _____

B. Correcting a mistake while typing [E 1.17]

Use the BACKSPACE key to _____

Use the ESC key to _____

C. AutoCorrect [E 1.18]

The AutoCorrect feature corrects _____

AutoCorrect makes three types of corrections:

     1. _____

     2. _____

     3. _____

D. Entering column titles [E 1.18]

   ☞ To enter the column titles

     1. _____

     2. _____

     3. _____

     4. _____

If the next entry is in an adjacent cell, use _____

If the next entry is in a non-adjacent cell, click _____

E. Entering row titles [E 1.19]

   ☞ To enter the row titles

     1. _____

     2. _____

VII.   Entering numbers [E 1.20]

Numbers can contain _____

☞ To enter numeric data

1.   _____

2.   _____

Numbers are right-aligned, which means _____

3.   _____

VIII. Calculating a sum [E 1.22]

Excel's SUM function provides _____

The AutoSum button on the Standard toolbar is used to _____

☞ To sum a column of numbers

1.   _____

2.   _____

3.   _____

A range is _____

IX.   Using the fill handle to copy a cell to adjacent cells [E 1.24]

A function can be copied from one cell to another cell or to a range of cells.

•   The copy area is _____

•   The paste area is _____

When you copy cell references, Excel adjusts them for each new position.

A relative reference is _____

The fill handle is _____

☞ To copy a cell to adjacent cells in a row

1.   _____

2.   _____

3.   _____

See-through view is _____

A. Determining row totals [E 1.25]

☞ To determine multiple totals at the same time

1.   _____

2.   _____

3.   _____

4.   _____

X. Formatting the worksheet [E 1.27]

You format a worksheet to _____

A. Fonts, font size, and font style [E 1.28]

- The font type defines _____

- The font size specifies _____

  Font size is gauged in points. A single point ≈ _____

  Point size is _____

- Font style indicates _____

B. Displaying the Formatting toolbar in its entirety [E 1.28]

☞ To display the Formatting toolbar in its entirety

1. _____

C. Bolding a cell [E 1.28]

You bold an entry to _____

☞ To bold a cell

1. _____

2. _____

D. Increasing the font size [E 1.30]

☞ To increase the font size of a cell entry

1. _____

2. _____

E. Using AutoFormat to format the body of a worksheet [E 1.31]

The AutoFormat command on the Format menu can be used to format a range automatically.

☞ To use AutoFormat to format the body of a worksheet

1. _____

_____

2. _____

3. _____

4. _____

AutoFormat dialog box buttons:

- The Close button allows you to _____

- The Cancel button is used to _____

- The OK button allows you to _____

- The Question Mark button obtains _____

- The Options button allows you to _____

F. Centering the worksheet title across columns [E 1.33]

☞ To center a cell's contents across columns

1. _____

    _____

2. _____

3. _____

Most formats assigned to a cell will display _____

XI. Using the Name box to select a cell [E 1.34]

The Name box is _____

☞ To use the Name box to select a cell

1. _____

2. _____

XII. Adding a 3-D Column chart to the worksheet [E 1.36]

An embedded chart is _____

Click the Chart Wizard button to _____

The chart location is _____

☞ To add a 3-D Column chart to the worksheet

1. _____

    _____

2. _____

3. _____

    _____

4. _____

    Sizing handles indicate _____

5. _____

    _____

6. _____

7. _____

    _____

8. _____

    _____

The y-axis or value axis (vertical axis) scale is derived _____

The x-axis or category axis (horizontal axis) titles are _____

The legend identifies _____

The default chart type is _____

XIII. Saving a workbook [E 1.41]

If power is turned off or lost, a workbook in the computer's memory is lost. Any workbook that will be used later must be stored on a floppy disk or hard disk.

A file or workbook is _____

☞ To save a workbook

  1. _____

  2. _____

  3. _____

  4. _____

  5. _____

    The .xls extension is _____

In the Save As dialog box:

• Clicking the Tools button displays _____

• The General Options command allows you to _____

 _____

  ○ A backup workbook means _____

  ○ A password is assigned so _____

    A password is case sensitive, meaning _____

• Clicking the History button displays _____

XIV. Printing the worksheet [E 1.45]

A hard copy or printout is _____

☞ To print a worksheet

  1. _____

  2. _____

XV. Quitting Excel [E 1.46]

☞ To quit Excel

  1. _____

  2. _____

  3. _____

XVI. Starting Excel and opening a workbook [E 1.47]

☞ To start Excel and open a workbook

  1. _____

  2. _____

  3. _____

XVII. AutoCalculate [E 1.49]

  The AutoCalculate area can be used to _____

  ☞ To use the AutoCalculate area to determine an average

    1. _____

    2. _____

    3. _____

XVIII. Correcting errors [E 1.51]

  The method you choose to correct errors will depend on _____

  _____

  A. Correcting errors while you are typing data into a cell [E 1.51]

    If you notice an error while typing data into a cell _____

    _____

  B. In-cell editing [E 1.51]

    If you notice an error after entering data into a cell

    1. If the entry is short _____

    _____

    2. If the entry is long and errors are minor, use Edit mode.

     (a) In-cell editing is _____

      _____

     (b) Make your changes.

      (1) To insert characters _____

       _____

      (2) To delete characters _____

       _____

       _____

       Click the Cut button to _____

      (3) When you are finished _____

    The INSERT key toggles the keyboard between Insert mode and Overtype mode.

    • In Insert mode _____

    • In Overtype mode _____

  C. Undoing the last entry [E 1.52]

    The Undo command on the Edit menu and the Undo button on the Standard toolbar can be

    used to _____

    The Redo button allows you to _____

D.   Clearing a cell or range of cells   [E 1.53]

Never press the SPACEBAR to _____

   ☞   To clear cell contents using the fill handle

      1. _____

      2. _____

   ☞   To clear cell contents using the shortcut menu

      1. _____

      2. _____

      3. _____

   ☞   To clear cell contents using the DELETE key

      1. _____

      2. _____

   ☞   To clear cell contents using the Clear command

      1. _____

      2. _____

      3. _____

The Cut button or Cut command allow you to _____

E.   Clearing the entire worksheet   [E 1.54]

   ☞   To clear the entire worksheet

      1. _____

      2. _____

The Select All button selects _____

Click the Close button or Close on the File menu to _____

Click the New button or New on the File menu to _____

   ☞   To delete an embedded chart

      1. _____

      2. _____

XIX.   Excel Help system   [E 1.54]

The Excel Help system can be used to _____

A.   Using the Office Assistant   [E 1.54]

The Office Assistant answers _____

IntelliSense™ technology is _____

   ☞   To obtain Help using the Office Assistant

      1. _____

      _____

2. _____

3. _____

4. _____

B. Quitting Excel [E 1.57]

☞ To quit Excel

1. _____

2. _____

Review

Matching (5)

Match each key or key combination on the left with the best description from the right.

____ 1. ALT+PAGE DOWN

____ 2. CTRL+ARROW

____ 3. CTRL+HOME

____ 4. HOME

____ 5. PAGE DOWN

a. selects the cell one window to the right and moves the window accordingly

b. selects cell A1 or the cell one column and one row below and to the right of frozen titles and moves the window accordingly

c. selects the cell one window to the left and moves the window accordingly

d. selects the border cell of the worksheet in combination with the arrow keys and moves the window accordingly

e. selects the cell up one window from the active cell and moves the window accordingly

f. selects the cell at the beginning of the row that contains the active cell and moves the window accordingly

g. selects the cell down one window from the active cell and moves the window accordingly

True/False (10)

*Circle **T** if the statement is true and **F** if the statement is false.*

T **F**   1. A new Excel workbook opens with 255 worksheets.

T **F**   2. Each worksheet in a workbook has 256 columns and 65,536 rows for a total of 16,777,216 cells.

T **F**   3. To identify a cell, specify the row number first, followed by the column letter.

T **F**   4. You can drag the tab split box to increase or decrease the view of the sheet tabs.

T **F**   5. In Excel, text is right-aligned unless you change it by realigning it.

T **F**   6. When proposing a range to sum, Excel first looks for a range of cells with numbers below the active cell and then to the right.

T **F**   7. When you copy cell references, Excel automatically adjusts them for each new location.

T **F**   8. When Excel begins, the preset font type for the entire workbook is Times New Roman with a size and style of 12-point bold.

T **F**   9. If you assign a password to a workbook and then forget the password, you cannot access the workbook.

T **F** 10. Press the SPACEBAR to clear a selected cell.

Definitions (5)

Briefly define each term.

1. cell _____

2. Chart menu bar _____

3.   range _____

4.   legend _____

5.   print area _____

The Excel Screen (5)

Identify the elements indicated in Figure E1.

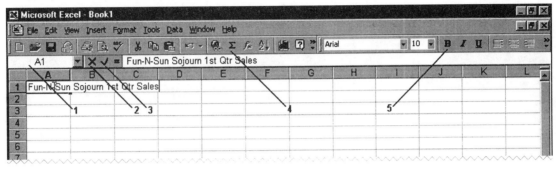

Figure E1

1. _____   4. _____

2. _____   5. _____

3. _____

Multiple Choice (5)

Circle the letter of the best answer.

1.   What is *not* a way that the active cell can be identified?
    a.   a heavy border surrounds the cell
    b.   the active cell reference displays in the Name box
    c.   the cell's column heading and row heading "light up"
    d.   the mouse pointer changes to a block plus sign when in the cell

2.   Although gridlines can be turned off, why is it recommended that you leave them on?
    a.   they display names that represent lists of commands to manipulate data
    b.   they can be used to move the window around to view different parts of a worksheet
    c.   they make it easier to see and identify each cell in a worksheet
    d.   they contain buttons and list boxes to perform frequents tasks more quickly

3.   When using the SUM function, how can you enter the correct range by typing?
    a.   type the beginning cell reference, a hyphen (-),and the ending cell reference
    b.   type the beginning cell reference, a colon (:), and the ending cell reference
    c.   type the beginning cell reference, a slash (/), and the ending cell reference
    d.   type the beginning cell reference, an asterisk (*), and the ending cell reference

4.   When you install Excel on a computer, what is the default chart type?
    a.   3-D (three-dimensional) Pie chart
    b.   2-D (two-dimensional) Line chart
    c.   3-D (three-dimensional) Scatter chart
    d.   2-D (two-dimensional) Column chart

5. When should you use the Contents sheet to obtain Help?
    a. when you know only the general category of the topic in question
    b. when you know the first few letters of the term or the exact term you want to find
    c. when you know a word located somewhere in the word or phrase you want to look up
    d. when you want to display ScreenTips concerning items in the Excel window

Dialog Box (5)

Answer the following questions about the AutoFormat dialog box shown in Figure E2.

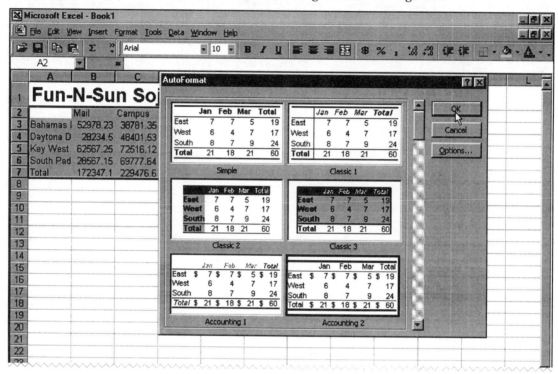

Figure E2

1. How was the dialog box displayed? _____

2. What format is selected? _____

3. How would you display more formats? _____

4. How can you terminate the current activity without making changes? _____

5. What does the Options button do? _____

Fill in the Blanks (5)

Write a word (or words) in the blank to complete each sentence correctly.

1. A cell is referred to by its unique address, or _____, which is the coordinates of the intersection of a column and a row.

2. The easiest way to _____ a cell (make it active) is to use the mouse to move the block plus sign to the cell and then click.

3. To cancel an entire entry before entering it into a cell, click the Cancel box in the formula bar or press the _____.

4. A character with a(n) _____ of 10 is about 10/72 of one inch in height.

5. Small _____ at the corners and along the sides of the selection rectangle indicate the chart is selected.

Sequence (5)

Use the numbers 1 – 5 to show the order in which these steps should be performed to use AutoFormat to format the body of a worksheet.

____ Drag the mouse pointer to the cell in the lower-right corner of the range to format.

____ Click the OK button. Select a cell outside the range to deselect the formatted range.

____ Click Format on the menu bar and then point to AutoFormat.

____ Select the cell in the upper-left corner of the rectangular range to format.

____ Click AutoFormat. Click the desired format in the AutoFormat dialog box.

Short Answer (5)

Write a brief answer to each question.

1. How is a short menu different from a full menu? How can you display a full menu?

2. When text is longer than the width of a column, what happens to the overflow characters? When you complete an entry by clicking the Enter box, what cell becomes the active cell?

3. Why do people save a backup workbook? Why is a password assigned to a workbook?

4. How is Insert mode different from Overtype mode? How do you toggle between the two modes?

5. How is clearing cell contents using the Cut button or Cut command different from clearing cell contents using the DELETE key? How can you clear formats of a selected range?

Activities

Use Help

Use Help to answer each question.

1. How can you **display multiple lines of text** within a cell? Use the Office Assistant to find out.

2. How do you go about **changing the font and colors of Help topics**? Look in the Getting Help book on the Contents sheet to find out.

3. How can you **change the default chart type**? Use the Index sheet to find out.

Expanding on the Lab

Perform the following tasks.

1. Open the Marvin's Music & Movie Mirage worksheet created in In the Lab 1.

2. Reformat the worksheet title, Gulliver's Travels Bookstore, as 14-point Book Antiqua bold.

3. Change Web sales for CDs to $21,740.20.

4. Change Telephone sales for Tapes to $9,897.32.

5. Change Mail Order sales for DVDs to $53,897.31.

6. Reformat the range A2:F8 using the AutoFormat command. Use the format Classic 3.

7. Move the chart so that two rows (rows 9 and 10) display between the chart and the table.

8. Print the modified worksheet.

9. Close the workbook without saving the changes.

Puzzle

Use the clues below to complete the crossword puzzle.

Creating a Worksheet

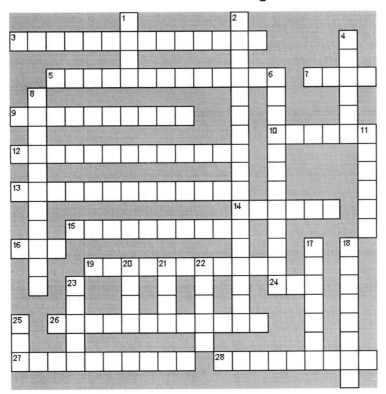

Across

3. Powerful spreadsheet program.
5. Chart drawn on the same worksheet as the data.
7. Saved workbook.
9. Displays data as it is typed.
10. Identifies each bar in a chart.
12. Coordinates of the intersection of a column and a row.
13. Area on the status bar that can be used in place of a calculator.
14. Done to emphasize certain worksheet entries.
15. Small black square located in the lower right corner of the active cell border.
16. Type of heading to the left of the worksheet grid.
19. Excel feature that automatically remedies common mistakes.
24. Function that totals the numbers in a range of cells.
26. Position of numbers in a cell.
27. View with a heavy border and transparent (blue) background.
28. Displays a brief description of the selected command or current activity.

Down

1. Font style assigned to an entry to make it stand out.
2. Adjusted cell reference.
4. Type of heading above the worksheet grid.
6. Customized format styles.
8. Toolbar button used to display buttons that are hidden.
11. Type of command that is not available for the current selection.
17. Can include only these characters: 0 1 2 3 4 5 6 7 8 9 + - ( ) , / . $ % E e.
18. Displays each worksheet name at the bottom of a workbook.
20. Any set of characters containing a letter, hyphen, or space.
21. Basic unit of a worksheet into which data is entered.
22. Series of two or more adjacent cells.
23. About 1/72 of one inch in height.
25. Extension automatically appended to workbook file name.

Microsoft Excel 2000

Project Two
Formulas, Functions, Formatting, and Web Queries

Overview

In creating the workbook in this project, you learn how to enter formulas, calculate an average, find the highest and lowest numbers in a range, audit formulas, change fonts, draw borders, format numbers, change column widths and row heights, and add conditional formatting to a range of numbers. Spell checking a worksheet, previewing a worksheet, printing a worksheet, printing a section of a worksheet, and displaying and printing the formulas in the worksheet using the Fit to option are explained. You discover how to complete a Web query to generate a worksheet using external data obtained from the World Wide Web and rename sheet tabs. Finally, you learn how to send an e-mail directly from within Excel with the opened workbook attached.

Project Outline

    I. Introduction [E 2.4]
       This Project introduces formulas, verifying formulas, changing fonts, adding borders, formatting numbers, conditional formatting, changing column widths and row heights, spell checking, e-mailing from within an application, and alternative types of worksheet displays and printouts.

    II. Project Two – BetNet Stock Club [E 2.4]

       A. Starting Excel and resetting the toolbars [E 2.6]

         ☞ To start Excel and reset the toolbars

          1. _____

          2. _____

          3. _____

          4. _____

          5. _____

          6. _____

    III. Entering titles and numbers into the worksheet [E 2.7]

       ☞ To enter the worksheet title

         1. _____

         2. _____

       Press ALT+ENTER to _____

☞ To enter the column titles

1. _____
2. _____
3. _____
4. _____
5. _____
6. _____
7. _____
8. _____
9. _____
10. _____

☞ To enter the stock data

1. _____
2. _____
3. _____
4. _____

☞ To enter the total row titles

1. _____
2. _____

IV. Entering formulas [E 2.9]

A formula is a symbolic representation of the relationship between changing values. One of the reasons Excel is a valuable tool is that you can _____

☞ To enter a formula using the keyboard

1. _____
2. _____

The equal sign (=) is an important part of the formula because _____

_____

Valid arithmetic operators include:

-	_____	%	_____
^	_____	*	_____
/	_____	+	_____
-	_____		

A. Order of operations [E 2.10]

Moving from left to right in a formula, the order of operations is _____

_____

You can use parentheses to _____

B. Entering formulas using Point mode [E 2.11]

Point mode allows you to _____

☞ To enter formulas using Point mode

1. _____

2. _____

3. _____

4. _____

C. Copying formulas using the fill handle [E 2.12]

☞ To copy formulas using the fill handle

1. _____

2. _____

3. _____

Relative references are _____

D. Determining the totals using the AutoSum button [E 2.14]

☞ To determine totals using the AutoSum button

1. _____

2. _____

E. Determining the total percentage gain/loss [E 2.15]

☞ To determine total percentage gain/loss

1. _____

2. _____

A blank cell has a numerical value of _____

V. Using the AVERAGE, MAX, and MIN functions [E 2.16]

Functions are _____

• Arguments are _____

You can enter functions using one of three methods:

1. _____

2. _____

3. _____

A. Determining the average of a range of numbers [E 2.16]

The AVERAGE function sums _____

☞ To determine the average of a range of numbers using the keyboard and mouse

1. _____

_____

2. _____

B. Determining the highest number in a range of numbers [E 2.18]

The MAX function displays _____

☞ To determine the highest number in a range of numbers using the Edit Formula box and

Functions box

1. _____

_____

The Functions box contains _____

The Formula Palette displays _____

2. _____

3. _____

C. Determining the lowest number in a range of numbers [E 2.20]

The MIN function determines _____

Click Excel's Paste Function button to _____

☞ To determine the lowest number in a range of numbers using the Paste Function button

1. _____

2. _____

_____

3. _____

D. Copying the AVERAGE, MAX, and MIN functions [E 2.21]

☞ To copy a range of cells across columns to an adjacent range using the fill handle

1. _____

_____

2. _____

3. _____

4. _____

_____

VI. Verifying formulas [E 2.23]

One of the most common mistakes is to include the wrong cell references in a formula.

• Auditing commands allow _____

○ The Trace Precedents command highlights _____

_____

○ The Trace Dependents command highlights _____

_____

○ The Remove All Arrows command removes _____

- Range Finder can be used to _____
  _____

A. Verifying a formula using Range Finder [E 2.24]

　　☞　To verify a formula using Range Finder

　　　　1. _____

　　　　2. _____

B. Verifying a formula using the Auditing commands [E 2.24]

　　☞　To verify a formula using the Auditing commands

　　　　1. _____
　　　　　 _____

　　　　2. _____

　　　　3. _____
　　　　　 _____

　　　　4. _____

　　To change the active cell to the one at the other end of the blue line _____

VII. Formatting the worksheet [E 2.26]

A. Changing the font and centering the worksheet title [E 2.28]

　　☞　To change the font and center the worksheet title

　　　　1. _____
　　　　　 _____

　　　　2. _____

　　　　3. _____

　　　　4. _____
　　　　　 _____

B. Changing the worksheet title background and font colors and applying an outline border [E 2.30]

　　☞　To change the title background and font colors and apply an outline border

　　　　1. _____
　　　　　 _____

　　　　2. _____
　　　　　 _____

　　　　3. _____
　　　　　 _____

　　　　4. _____

Remove borders by _____

Remove a background color by _____

Change font color back to black by _____

C. Applying formats to the column titles [E 2.32]

☞ To bold, center, and underline the column titles

1. _____
   _____

2. _____

D. Centering the stock symbols and formatting the numbers in the worksheet [E 2.33]

☞ To center data in cells

1. _____

The Cells command on the Format menu or the Format Cells command on the shortcut menu

is used to _____

• The Currency style format displays _____
  _____

• The Currency style button assigns _____

   o   A fixed dollar sign displays _____

   o   A floating dollar sign displays _____

• The Comma style format inserts _____
  _____

E. Formatting numbers using the Formatting toolbar [E 2.35]

☞ To apply a Currency style format and Comma style format using the Formatting toolbar

1. _____
   _____

2. _____

3. _____
   _____

4. _____
   _____

The Increase Decimal button displays _____

The Decrease Decimal button removes _____

F. Formatting numbers using the Format Cells command on the shortcut menu [E 2.36]

☞ To apply a Currency style with a floating dollar sign using the Format Cells command

1. _____

2. _____
   _____

3. _____

G. Formatting numbers using the Percent Style button and Increase Decimal button [E 2.39]

☞ To apply a Percentage format

1. _____

2. _____

The Percent Style button displays _____

_____

The Conditional Formatting command is used to _____

_____

H. Conditional formatting [E 2.40]

Conditional formatting is _____

A condition is _____

☞ To apply conditional formatting

1. _____

2. _____

_____

3. _____

_____

4. _____

5. _____

In the Conditional Formatting dialog box:

• The Preview window shows _____

• The Add button allows _____

• The Delete button allows _____

I. Changing the widths of columns and heights of rows [E 2.43]

Excel's default column width is 8.43 characters, or 64 pixels.

• A character is _____

• A pixel is _____

Excel's default row height is 12.75 points, or 17 pixels.

• A point is _____

J. Changing the width of columns [E 2.43]

Best fit means _____

Excel allows column widths to be changed manually.

☞ To change the width of a column by dragging

1. _____

_____

2. _____

_____

3. _____

_____

4. _____

_____

5. _____

Hiding is _____

To hide a column _____

To display a hidden column _____

K. Changing the heights of rows [E 2.46]

☞ To change the height of a row by dragging

1. _____

2. _____

_____

3. _____

_____

Like columns, rows can be hidden.

VIII. Checking spelling [E 2.48]

Excel's spell checker looks for errors by comparing words against words contained in its standard
dictionary.

☞ To check spelling in a worksheet

1. _____

_____

2. _____

3. _____

In the Spelling dialog box:

- The Change to box displays _____

- The Suggestions list displays _____

- Click the Change button to _____

- Click the Change All button to _____

- Click the Ignore button to _____

- Click the Ignore All button to _____

- Click the Add button to _____

- Click the AutoCorrect button to _____

IX. Saving the workbook a second time using the same file name [E 2.50]

To save a workbook a second time using the same file name _____

Click Save on the File menu to _____

Click Save As on the File menu to _____

X. Previewing and printing the worksheet [E 2.51]

- Portrait orientation means _____

- Landscape orientation means _____

Use the Print Preview command on the File menu or the Print Preview button on the Standard

toolbar to _____

☞ To preview and print a worksheet

1. _____

2. _____

3. _____

_____

4. _____

5. _____

6. _____

A. Printing a section of the worksheet [E 2.54]

☞ To print a section of the worksheet

1. _____

_____

2. _____

In the Print what area of the Print dialog box:

- The Selection option button instructs _____

- The Active sheet(s) option button instructs _____

- The Entire workbook option button instructs _____

XI. Displaying and printing the formulas version of the worksheet [E 2.55]

- The values version shows _____

- The formulas version displays _____

The formulas version of a worksheet is useful for debugging. Debugging is _____

_____

To toggle between values version and formulas version, press _____

The Fit to option can be used to _____

☞ To display the formulas in a worksheet and fit the printout on one page

1. _____

2. _____

_____

3. _____

_____

A. Changing the print scaling option back to 100% [E 2.57]

☞ To change the print scaling option back to 100%

1. _____

2. _____

3. _____

4. _____

The Adjust to box allows _____

XII. Getting external data from a Web source using a Web query [E 2.58]

You can run a Web query to _____

☞ To get external data from a Web source using a Web query

1. _____

_____

2. _____

_____

3. _____

_____

4. _____

_____

5. _____

On the External Data toolbar:

• Click the Refresh All button to _____

• Click the Query Parameters button to _____

XIII. Changing the sheet names [E 2.61]

In a more sophisticated workbook, changing the names on the sheet tabs makes it easier to move among multiple sheets.

☞ To rename the sheets

1. _____

_____

2. _____

_____

3. _____

The tab split box can be dragged _____

Tab scrolling buttons can be used to _____

XIV. E-mailing a workbook from within Excel [E 2.62]

Using e-mail you can _____

☞ To e-mail a workbook from within Excel

     1. _____

         _____

     2. _____

     3. _____

         _____

     4. _____

XV. Quitting Excel [E 2.64]

☞ To quit Excel

     1. _____

     2. _____

     3. _____

Review

Matching (5)

If the value in cell B2 is 30, the value in cell B3 is 4, the value in cell C2 is 10, the value in cell C3 is 8, and the value in cell D2 is 2, match each formula on the left with its numerical equivalent on the right.

___	1.	=B2 + B3 * C3 - C2 / D2
___	2.	=C2 ^ 2 – B2 / D2 – B3 * C3
___	3.	=D2 * C3 + B3 * B2 / C2
___	4.	=B2 – B3 ^ 2 / C3 + C2 * D2
___	5.	=C3 * C2 – B3 ^ D2 - B2

a. 53

b. 48

c. 28

d. 54

e. 57

f. 62

g. 34

True/False (10)

*Circle **T** if the statement is true and **F** if the statement is false.*

T   **F**   1.   Press CTRL+ENTER to start a new line in a cell.

T   **F**   2.   A function takes a value or values, performs an operation, and returns a value or values.

T   **F**   3.   All functions begin with an equal sign and include the arguments in parentheses after the function name.

T   **F**   4.   A caret (^) at the beginning of an entry instructs Excel to left-align the text.

T   **F**   5.   When the format you assign to a cell causes the entry to exceed the width of a column, Excel automatically changes the column width to best fit.

T   **F**   6.   If you decrease column width to zero, the column is hidden.

T   **F**   7.   To check the spelling of the text in a single cell, select the cell so that the formula bar is not active and then start the spell checker.

T   **F**   8.   You can click Save on the File menu or press SHIFT+F12 or CTRL+S to re-save a workbook.

T   **F**   9.   The Print dialog box displays when you use the Print button on the Standard toolbar.

T   **F**   10.   You can toggle between the values version and formulas version of a worksheet by pressing CTRL+` (left single quotation mark to the left of the number 1 key).

Definitions (5)

Briefly define each term.

1. point mode _____

2. arguments _____

3. conditional formatting _____

4. pixels _____

5. best fit _____

The Excel Screen (5)

Explain the function of each of the Print Preview buttons indicated in Figure E3.

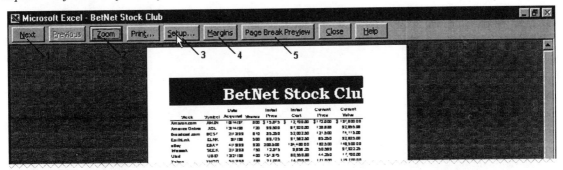

Figure E 3

1. _____

2. _____

3. _____

4. _____

5. _____

Multiple Choice (5)

Circle the letter of the best answer.

1. Which of the following formulas would have the same numerical value as =C2 + D2 * E2 – F2?
   a. =(C2 + D2) * E2 – F2
   b. =C2 + D2 * (E2 – F2)
   c. =C2 + (D2 * E2) – F2
   d. =(C2 + D2) * (E2 – F2)

2. When determining the highest value in a range, what advantage does entering the MAX function have over simply scanning the range and entering the largest value as a constant?
   a. Excel recalculates the highest value each time you enter a new value in the range
   b. it usually is easier to enter a function than it is to enter a number accurately
   c. Excel does not change the result of a function, even if other values in a worksheet are altered
   d. functions can be entered using Point mode, but numbers only can be entered using the keyboard

3. Before adding a percent sign, how is the value displayed in a cell determined when the Percent Style button on the Formatting toolbar is clicked?
   a. by adding 100 to the cell entry and rounding the result to the nearest percent
   b. by subtracting 100 from the cell entry and rounding the result to the nearest percent
   c. by multiplying the cell entry by 100 and rounding the result to the nearest percent
   d. by dividing the cell entry by 100 and rounding the result to the nearest percent

4. How is saving the workbook a second time by clicking the Save button on the Standard toolbar different from saving the workbook again by clicking Save As on the File menu?
   a. clicking the Save button automatically saves the workbook with the same file name
   b. clicking Save As automatically saves the workbook with the same file name
   c. clicking the Save button displays a dialog box that lets you save the workbook using a new name or to a different drive
   d. clicking Save As displays a dialog box that lets you save the workbook using a new name or to a different drive

5. To e-mail a workbook from within Excel, you must have an e-mail address and what for your e-mail program?
    a. Outlook
    b. Outlook Express
    c. Microsoft Exchange Client
    d. any of the above

Dialog Box (5)

Answer the following questions about the Print dialog box shown in Figure E4.

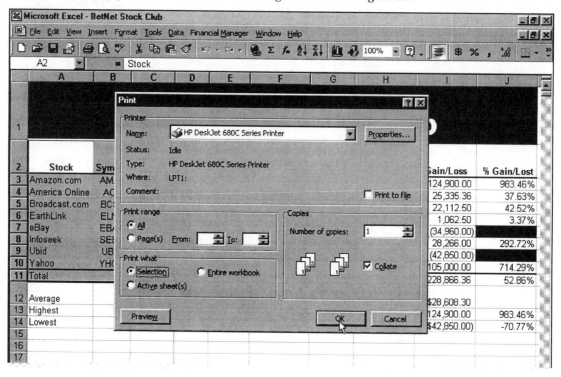

Figure E4

1. How was the dialog box displayed? _____

2. What printer will be used? _____

3. What part of the worksheet will be printed? _____

4. How would you print just the entire worksheet? _____

5. How many copies will be printed? _____

Fill in the Blanks (5)

Write a word (or words) in the blank to complete each sentence correctly.

1. Excel includes prewritten formulas called _____ that help you compute statistics.

2. Customized formats can be assigned using the _____ on the Format menu.

3. A(n) _____ is defined as a letter, number, symbol, or punctuation mark in 10-point Arial font, the default font used by Excel.

4. _____ is the process of finding and correcting errors in a worksheet.

5. You can run a(n) _____ to retrieve data stored on a World Wide Web site.

Sequence (5)

Use the numbers 1 – 5 to show the order in which these steps should be performed to enter a simple formula using Point mode.

____   Click the Enter box or press the ENTER key.

____   Click the second cell in the formula.

____   Type an arithmetic operator.

____   Click the first cell in the formula.

____   With the cell where the formula will be entered selected, type = (equal sign).

Short Answer (5)

Write a brief answer to each question.

1. Why does the ability to assign a formula to a cell make Excel a valuable tool? What advantage does entering a formula have over entering specific values?

2. How do Auditing commands and Range Finder help to verify the accuracy of formulas? What is an advantage of Range Finder?

3. How is a fixed dollar sign different from a floating dollar sign? Which is applied by the Currency Style button on the Formatting toolbar?

4. How is Portrait orientation different from Landscape orientation? In what orientation does Excel print a new (unsaved) workbook? In what orientation does Excel print a saved workbook?

5. How is the values version of a worksheet different from the formulas version? Why is the formulas version useful for debugging a worksheet?

Activities

Use Help

Use Help to answer each question.

1. How can you use the Auditing commands to **locate cells that cause errors in a formula**? Use the Office Assistant to find out.

2. What does the error message **#DIV/0!** mean? What are possible causes of the error? Use the Index sheet to find out.

3. How does Microsoft Excel handle **dates in the year 2000 and beyond**? Look in the Year 2000 Issues book on the Contents sheet to find out.

Expanding on the Lab

Perform the following tasks.

1. Open the Stars and Stripes Automotive workbook created in In the Lab 1.

2. Increase the rate of pay for each employee by $2.00.

3. Change the formula for State Tax (cell G3) to =3.2% * Gross Pay or =3.2% * E3.

4. Use Range Finder and then the Auditing commands to verify the formula entered in cell G3. Check both precedents and dependents with the Auditing commands. Remove all arrows.

5. Use the Conditional Formatting command on the Format menu to display bold font on a red background for any net pay less than $825 in the range H3:H8.

6. Preview and then print the worksheet.

7. Display the formulas version of the worksheet. Print the formulas version of the worksheet in landscape orientation using the Fit to option on the Page tab in the Page Setup dialog box.

8. Close the workbook without saving any changes.

ACTIVITIES E 2.17

Puzzle

The terms described by the phrases below are written below each line in code. Break the code by writing the correct term above the coded word. Then, use your broken code to translate the final sentences.

1. Key combination used to start a new line in a cell.

   _____
   ZHD+XGDXE

2. Recalculated whenever new values are entered.

   _____
   KSETPHZ

3. Used to override the order of operations.

   _____
   FZEXGDJXQXQ

4. Allows cells for use in a formula to be selected by using the mouse.

   _____
   FSVGD TSLX

5. Prewritten formulas used to help compute statistics.

   _____
   KPGYDVSGQ

6. Values used with a function.

   _____
   ZEWPTXGDQ

7. Determines the arithmetic mean of a range.

   _____
   ZCXEZWX KPGYDVSG

8. Standard toolbar button used to enter a function.

   _____
   FZQDX KPGYDVSG

9. Shortcut menu command used to assign customized formats.

   _____
   KSETZD YXHHQ

10. Format that displays a dollar sign to the left of a number.

    _____
    YPEEXGYN QDNHX

11. Format that inserts a comma every three positions to the left of the decimal point.

    _____
    YSTTZ QDNHX

12. Made up of two values and a relational operator.

    _____
    YSGLVDVSG

13. A letter, number, symbol, or punctuation mark in 10-point TT Arial font.

    _____
    YJZEZYDXE

14. Short for picture element, a dot on the screen that contains a color.

    _____
    FVBXH

15. Means that column width changes automatically to accommodate the widest entry.

    _____
    MXQD KVD

16. Technique used to conceal irrelevant or sensitive data.

    _____
    JVLVGW

17. Spelling dialog box button used to skip correcting a word.

    _____
    VWGSEX

18. Worksheet version that shows the results of formulas entered, rather than the formulas.

    _____
    CZHPXQ

19. Preview window button that magnifies or reduces the print preview.

_____
ASST

20. Can be used with landscape orientation to keep a wide printout on one page.

_____
KVD DS SFDVSG

ZG VGGSCZDVCX KXZDPEX SK XBYXH 2000 VQ DJX ZCZVHZMVHVDN SK

ZLLVDVSGZH GPTMXE KSETZDQ OVDJ DJX GXO XPES YPEEXGYN QNTMSH.

Microsoft Excel 2000

Project Three
What-If Analysis, Charting, and Working with Large Worksheets

Overview

In creating the workbook for this project, you learn how to work with large worksheets that extend beyond the window and how to use the fill handle to create a series. You display hidden toolbars, dock a toolbar at the bottom of the screen, and hide an active toolbar. The difference between absolute and relative cell references and how to use the IF function are explained. You discover how to rotate text in a cell, generate a series, freeze titles, change the magnification of the worksheet, display different parts of the worksheet through panes, and improve the appearance of a chart. Finally, this project introduces using Excel to do what-if analyzes by changing values in cells and goal seeking.

Project Outline

I.   Introduction [E 3.4]

The Drawing toolbar allows _____

Assumptions are _____

II. Project Three – Hyperlink.com Six-Month Projected Revenue, Expenses, and Net Income [E 3.6]

    A.   Starting Excel and resetting toolbars and menus [E 3.6]

        ☞ To start Excel and reset toolbars and menus

          1. _____

          2. _____

          3. _____

          4. _____

          5. _____

          6. _____

          7. _____

    B.   Changing the font of the entire worksheet to bold [E 3.7]

        ☞ To bold the font of the entire worksheet

          1. _____

          2. _____

    C.   Entering the worksheet titles [E 3.7]

☞ To enter the worksheet titles

1. _____

2. _____

3. _____

III. Rotating text and using the fill handle to create a series [E 3.8]

When you first enter text, its angle is zero degrees (0°), and it reads from left to right in a cell.

You rotate text counterclockwise by _____

_____

You can use the fill handle to create _____

☞ To rotate text and use the fill handle to create a series of month names

1. _____

_____

_____

2. _____

_____

3. _____

4. _____

5. _____

You can create several different types of series using the fill handle.

Examples of Series Using the Fill Handle			
CONTENTS OF CELL(S) COPIED	NEXT THREE VALUES IN SERIES	CONTENTS OF CELL(S) COPIED	NEXT THREE VALUES IN SERIES
3:00	_____	1, 2	_____
Qtr3	_____	600, 580	_____
Jul-2001, Oct-2001	_____	Sun	_____

Besides creating a series of values, the fill handle also copies the format of the initial cell.

IV. Copying a cell's format using the Format Painter button [E 3.10]

Use the Format Painter button on the Standard toolbar to _____

_____

☞ To copy a cell's format using the Format Painter button

1. _____

_____

2. _____

The Format Painter button also can be used to copy the formats of a cell to a range or to copy one range to another range.

A. Increasing the column widths and entering row titles [E 3.11]

☞ To increase column widths and enter row titles

1. _____
   _____

2. _____
   _____

3. _____
   _____
   _____

The Increase Indent button indents _____

The Decrease Indent button decreases _____

V. Copying a range of cells to a nonadjacent paste area [E 3.13]

The Copy button and the Copy command copy _____
_____

The Office Clipboard allows _____

The Clipboard toolbar displays _____

The Paste button and the Paste command copy _____
_____

To copy an older item on the Office Clipboard _____

☞ To copy a range of cells to a nonadjacent paste area

1. _____
   _____

2. _____

Click the Undo Paste command to _____

A. Using drag and drop to move or copy cells [E 3.15]

The mouse pointer changes to a block arrow when _____

Drag and drop is _____

Another way to move cells is to _____
_____

VI. Inserting and deleting cells in a worksheet

A. Inserting rows [E 3.16]

The Rows command on the Insert menu or the Insert command on the shortcut menu allow you to _____

☞ To insert rows

1. _____

2. _____

If shifted rows include formulas _____

The difference between the Insert command and the Rows command is _____

_____

B. Inserting columns [E 3.17]

You insert columns in the same way you insert rows.

The Columns command on the Insert menu requires _____

_____

C. Inserting individual cells or a range of cells [E 3.17]

The Cells command on the Insert menu or the Insert command on the shortcut menu allow

_____

It is recommended that only entire rows or columns be inserted to ensure _____

_____

D. Deleting columns and rows [E 3.18]

The Delete command on the Edit or shortcut menu removes _____

_____

Excel *does not* adjust cell references in formulas that reference deleted cells.

The error message #REF! indicates _____

E. Deleting individual cells or a range of cells [E 3.18]

It is recommended that _____

VII. Entering numbers with a format symbol [E 3.18]

When you enter a number with a format symbol _____

Valid format symbols include: _____

If the number entered with a format symbol:

- Is a whole number it displays _____

- Has decimal places it displays _____

☞ To enter a number with a format symbol

1. _____

_____

2. _____

_____

VIII. Freezing worksheet titles [E 3.19]

Freezing worksheet titles is a useful technique for _____

The Freeze Panes command on the Window menu _____

☞ To freeze column and row titles

    1. _____

    _____

    2. _____

Click the Unfreeze Panes command to _____

A. Entering the projected revenue [E 3.20]

☞ To enter the projected revenue

    1. _____

    2. _____

IX. Displaying the system date [E 3.21]

A date stamp shows _____

Use the NOW function to _____

☞ To enter and format the system date

    1. _____

    _____

    _____

    2. _____

    _____

    3. _____

    _____

    4. _____

If you assign the General format to a date _____

X. Absolute versus relative addressing [E 3.24]

Absolute referencing keeps _____

A mixed cell reference is _____

Examples of Cell References

CELL REFERENCE	TYPE OF REFERENCE	MEANING
$B$17	_____	_____
		_____

Examples of Cell References

CELL REFERENCE	TYPE OF REFERENCE	MEANING
B$17	_____	_____ _____
$B17	_____	_____ _____
B17	_____	_____ _____

A. Entering the July Administrative, Marketing, and Commission formulas [E 3.25]

☞ To enter formulas containing absolute cell references

1. _____
    _____

2. _____

3. _____
    _____
    _____

XI. Making decisions – the IF function [E 3.27]

The IF function is useful when _____

The general form of the IF function is _____

• value_if_true is _____

• value_if_false is _____

• A logical_test is _____

Valid comparison operators

COMPARISON OPERATOR	MEANING	COMPARISON OPERATOR	MEANING
=	_____	>=	_____
<	_____	<=	_____
>	_____	<>	_____

☞ To enter an IF function:

1. _____
    _____

2. _____

A. Entering the remaining projected expenses and net income formulas for July [E 3.29]

☞ To enter the remaining projected July expense and net income formulas

1. _____

2. _____

3. _____

4. _____

B. Copying the projected July expenses and net income formulas to the other months [E 3.30]

☞ To copy the projected July expenses and net income using the fill handle

1. _____

2. _____

C. Determining the projected total expenses by category and total net income [E 3.31]

☞ To determine the projected expenses by category and net income

1. _____

2. _____

D. Unfreezing worksheet titles and saving the workbook [E 3.32]

☞ To unfreeze the worksheet titles and save the workbook

1. _____

2. _____

3. _____

4. _____

XII. Formatting the worksheet [E 3.32]

A. Formatting the numbers [E 3.33]

The Format cells command must be used to _____

☞ To assign formats to the Projected Revenue, Expenses, and Net Income

1. _____

_____

_____

2. _____

_____

_____

3. _____

_____

_____

4. _____

In accounting, negative numbers often are displayed with _____

B. Formatting the worksheet titles [E 3.36]

☞ To format the worksheet titles

1. _____

_____

2. _____

3. _____

_____

4. _____

_____

5. _____

C. Displaying the Drawing toolbar [E 3.37]

The Drawing toolbar provides _____

The Toolbars command on the View menu can be used to _____

☞ To display the Drawing toolbar

1. _____

2. _____

D. Moving and docking a toolbar [E 3.38]

A floating toolbar displays _____

• To move a floating toolbar _____

• To hide a floating toolbar _____

A toolbar dock is _____

☞ To dock a toolbar at the bottom of the screen

1. _____

2. _____

E. Adding a drop shadow to the title area [E 3.39]

☞ To add a drop shadow

1. _____

_____

2. _____

F. Formatting the category row titles and Net Income row [E 3.40]

☞ To change font size, add background colors, and add drop shadows to nonadjacent
sections

1. _____

_____

2. _____
   _____
   _____

3. _____

G. Formatting the Assumptions table [E 3.42]

☞ To format the Assumptions table

1. _____
   _____
   _____

2. _____
   _____
   _____

3. _____
   _____

The italic font style slants _____

The underline format underlines _____

XIII. Adding a 3-D Pie chart to the workbook [E 3.43]

A Pie chart is _____

A chart sheet is _____

• Category names are _____

• The data series is _____

An exploded Pie chart is _____

A. Drawing a 3-D Pie chart on a separate chart sheet [E 3.44]

☞ To draw a 3-D Pie chart on a separate chart sheet

1. _____
   _____

2. _____
   _____

3. _____

4. _____
   _____

5. _____

6. _____

7. _____
   _____

8. _____

9. _____

Excel determines the direction of the data series range on the basis of the selected range.

B. Formatting the chart title and chart labels [E 3.49]

A chart item _____

☞ To format the chart title and labels

1. _____

_____

_____

2. _____

_____

_____

C. Changing the colors of the slices [E 3.50]

☞ To change the colors of the Pie slices

1. _____

_____

2. _____

_____

_____

D. Exploding the 3-D Pie chart [E 3.52]

Exploding is _____

☞ To explode the 3-D Pie chart

1. _____

2. _____

E. Rotating and tilting the 3-D Pie chart [E 3.52]

The 3-D View command on the Chart menu controls _____

_____

☞ To rotate and tilt the 3-D Pie chart

1. _____

2. _____

_____

3. _____

The Rotation box displays _____

4. _____

5. _____

The Height box controls _____

F. Adding leader lines to the data labels [E 3.55]

Leader lines connect _____

☞ To add leader lines to the data labels

1. _____

2. _____

_____

XIV. Changing the names of the sheets and rearranging the order of the sheets [E 3.56]

☞ To rename the sheets and rearrange the order of the sheets

1. _____

_____

2. _____

_____

XV. Checking spelling, saving, previewing, and printing the workbook [E 3.57]

A. Checking spelling in multiple sheets [E 3.57]

☞ To check spelling in multiple sheets

1. _____

2. _____

3. _____

B. Previewing and printing the workbook [E 3.57]

☞ To preview and print the workbook in landscape orientation

1. _____

2. _____

3. _____

4. _____

5. _____

6. _____

XVI. Changing the view of a worksheet [E 3.59]

Window panes can be used to _____

A. Shrinking and magnifying the view of a worksheet or chart [E 3.59]

The Zoom box is used to _____

☞ To shrink and magnify the view of a worksheet or chart

1. _____

2. _____

3. _____

      4. _____

         _____

      5. _____

B. Splitting the window into panes [E 3.61]

    The Split command on the Window menu is used to _____

    ☞ To split a window into four panes

        1. _____

           _____

        2. _____

    The vertical split bar is _____

    The horizontal split bar is _____

    ☞ To remove the four panes from the window

        1. _____

        2. _____

XVII. What-if analysis [E 3.63]

    What-if analysis or sensitivity analysis is _____

    _____

    ☞ To analyze data in a worksheet by changing values

        1. _____

        2. _____

           _____

        3. _____

XVIII. Goal seeking [E 3.65]

    Goal seeking is used to _____

    The Goal Seek command helps determine _____

    ☞ To goal seek

        1. _____

           _____

        2. _____

           _____

           _____

        3. _____

        4. _____

           _____

        5. _____

A. Quitting Excel [E 3.67]

    ☞ To quit Excel

        1. _____

        2. _____

Review

Matching (5)

Each formula on the left is copied from cell B5 to cell C6. Match each formula on the left with the formula from the right that would be entered in cell C6.

___ 1. =B3 + B4

___ 2. =$B$3 + $B$4

___ 3. =$B$3 + B4

___ 4. =$B3 + B4

___ 5. =B3 + B$4

a. =$B4 + C5

b. =C4 + C$4

c. =$B$3 + $B$4

d. =C4 + C5

e. =$C$4 + $C$5

f. =B$3 + C4

g. =$B$3 + C5

True/False (10)

*Circle **T** if the statement is true and **F** if the statement is false.*

T F   1. You can use the fill handle to create a series of numbers, dates, or month names.

T F   2. When you are copying the Clipboard contents to more than one nonadjacent cell or range, complete the copy by pressing the ENTER key.

T F   3. The Delete command clears the data from cells, but the cells remain in the worksheet.

T F   4. If formulas reference cells in a deleted row or column, Excel adjusts these cell references.

T F   5. If you assign the General format (Excel's default format for numbers) to the date, the date displays as a number.

T F   6. The general form of the IF function is: =IF(logical_test, value_if_false, value_if_true).

T F   7. You move a toolbar by pointing to a button (not to the title bar or to a blank area within the toolbar window) and then dragging the toolbar to its new location.

T F   8. Excel normally displays a chart at approximately 50% magnification so that the entire chart displays on the screen.

T F   9. Window panes split by the vertical split bar scroll together vertically.

T F 10. Goal seeking assumes you can change the value of multiple cells referenced either directly or indirectly.

Definitions (5)

Briefly define each term.

1. assumptions _____

2. drag and drop _____

3. date stamp _____

4. toolbar dock _____

5. italic _____

The Excel Screen (5)

Identify the elements indicated in Figure E5.

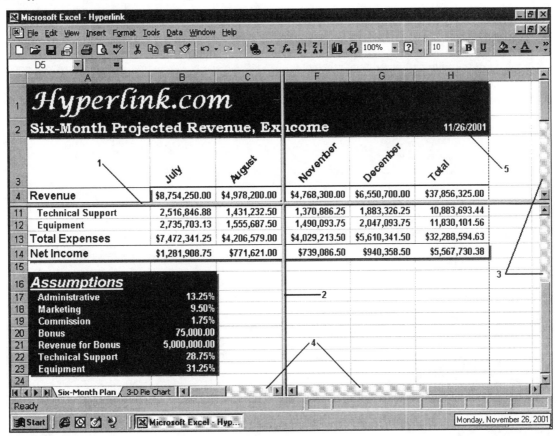

Figure E5

1. _____
2. _____
3. _____

4. _____
5. _____

Multiple Choice (5)

Circle the letter of the best answer.

1. If $1234.5 is typed in the formula bar, what displays in the cell?
   a. $1234.5
   b. $1,234.5
   c. $1234.50
   d. $1,234.50

2. What function is used to enter the system date in a worksheet cell?
   a. DATE
   b. DAYS360
   c. NOW
   d. TIME

3. Cell B4 contains the value 100, and cell D5 contains the value 90. When the function =IF(B4 ◇ D5, 80, 70) is entered in cell E7, what value will display in cell E7?
    a. 100
    b. 90
    c. 80
    d. 70

4. In which of the following would both the column and row references remain the same when you copy the cell reference?
    a. B16
    b. $B16
    c. B$16
    d. $B$16

5. What happens when you Zoom (magnify) a worksheet?
    a. the characters on the screen become small and fewer columns and rows display
    b. the characters on the screen become large and fewer columns and rows display
    c. the characters on the screen become small and more columns and rows display
    d. the characters on the screen become large and more columns and rows display

Formula Palette (5)

Answer the following questions about the Formula palette in the Figure E6.

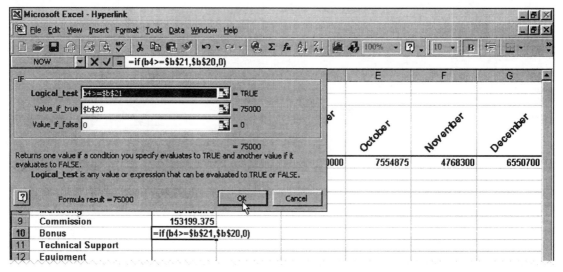

Figure E6

1. How do you display the Formula palette? _____

2. What Formula palette is shown? _____

3. The current value in cell B4 is 8754250 and the current value in cell and B21 5,000,000.00. Given these values, will the IF function result in a value of True or False? _____

4. What is the value_if_false? _____

5. What value will display as a result of this function? _____

Fill in the Blanks (5)

Write a word (or words) in the blank to correctly complete each sentence.

1. You can _____ counterclockwise by entering a number between 1° and 90° on the Alignment sheet in the Format Cells dialog box.

2. The mouse pointer changes to a(n) _____ when you are pointing to the border of a cell or range.

3. If cell A7 contains the formula =A4 + A5 and you delete row 5, then Excel displays the error message _____ in cell A6 (originally cell A7).

4. Excel's _____ function is useful when the value you want to assign to a cell is dependent on a logical test.

5. The _____ provides tools that can simplify adding lines, boxes, and other geometric figures to a worksheet.

Sequence (5)

Use the numbers 1 – 5 to show the order in which these steps should be performed to enter and format the system date.

____ Click the cell where the date will be entered and then click the Paste Function button on the Standard toolbar.

____ Click Format Cells on the shortcut menu and then click the Number tab in the Format Cells dialog box. Click Date in the Category list box and then click the desired format in the Type list box.

____ Click Date & Time in the Function category list box and then click NOW in the Function name list box.

____ Click the OK button.

____ Click the OK button. When the NOW Formula palette displays, click the OK button. Right-click the cell where the system date is displayed.

Short Answer (5)

Write a brief answer to each question.

1. When using the fill handle to create a series, for what types of series must you enter the first item in the series in one cell and the second item in the series in an adjacent cell? Why?

2. How do you copy formats to a range of cells?

3. How is pressing the ENTER key to complete a copy different from using the Paste button or the Paste command? When should you use the Paste button or Paste command instead of pressing the ENTER key?

4. Why is it recommended that you insert only entire rows or entire columns?

5. When drawing a 3-D Pie chart, how are the category names different from the data series? Why is it usually better not to offset multiple slices in a Pie chart.

Activities

Use Help

Use Help to answer each question.

1. Goal Seek and Solver are two ways to **forecast values with what-if analysis**. How are they different? On the Contents sheet, use an appropriate topic in the Saving Different Solutions to a Problem book in the Performing What-If Analysis on Worksheet Data book to find out.

2. Rows and columns can be hidden by decreasing the row height or column width to zero. How else can you **hide a row or column**? How do you **hide a workbook**? Use the Index sheet to find out.

3. How can you **resize a toolbar**? Use the Office Assistant to find out.

Expanding on the Lab

Perform the following tasks.

1. Open the R&R Hotel workbook created in In the Lab 1.

2. Click the Planned Indirect Expenses tab to display the worksheet.

3. A recently discovered leaky roof will require $8,000 worth of repairs . Increase the Projected Indirect Expenses for Maintenance (cell B21) to $32,000.

4. Change the Chart Type to Doughnut. (*Hint*: Start by right-clicking the chart sheet.)

5. Print the revised worksheet and chart.

6. Because the Dining Room must be closed for about five weeks while the leaky roof is repaired, R&R Hotel will be satisfied if the Dining Room's Net Income is $178,644.66 (90% of $198,494.07). Use the Goal Seek command to determine the Revenue (cell B4) necessary to achieve the desired Net Income (cell B15).

7. Print the resultant worksheet and chart.

8. Close the workbook without saving changes.

Puzzle

Write the word described by each clue in the puzzle below. Words can be written forward or backward, across, up and down, or diagonally. The first letter of each word already appears in the puzzle.

L							C	F	D
					C	U			
		💻	C		💻				
	💻		I					E	
	R							Z	
		💻							
			C		P				
I							💻		
N							💻		
						P			
		U		D				S	C
L									A

Values in cells that can be changed to determine new values for formulas.

Button that duplicates the contents and format of a selected range on the Office Clipboard.

Button that copies the newest item on the Office Clipboard to an area on the worksheet.

Edit menu command that reverses a paste.

Using the mouse to move or copy cells.

Insert menu command that allows rows to be inserted between rows that contain data.

Insert menu command that requires a single cell to be selected in a column to insert one column.

Insert menu command used to insert a single cell or a range of cells.

Edit menu command that removes cells from the worksheet.

Type of symbol that, when entered with a number, immediately displays the number with an assigned appearance.

Window menu command used to immobilize the worksheet title and column titles.

Function used to enter the system date.

Function useful when the value assigned to a cell is dependent on a logical test.

IF function entry made up of two expressions and a comparison operator.

Command used to assign a Currency style with a floating dollar sign.

Style that slants characters slightly to the right.

Format that underscores only the characters in a cell rather than the entire cell.

Type of chart used to show the relationship or proportion of parts to the whole.

Separate sheet on which a graph resides.

Element such as the chart title or labels that must be selected before it can be formatted.

Offsetting one slice from the rest of the slices in a Pie chart.

Thin links that connect each data label to its corresponding slice in a Pie chart.

Used to magnify or shrink the display of a worksheet.

Window menu command that divides the window into four panes.

Microsoft Excel 2000

Web Feature
Creating Static and Dynamic Web Pages Using Excel

Overview

This Web Feature introduces publishing two types of Web pages: static and dynamic. Whereas the static Web page is a snapshot of the workbook, a dynamic Web page adds functionality and interactivity to the Web page. Besides changing the data and generating new results with a dynamic Web page, you also can add formulas and change the formats in their browser to improve the appearance of the Web page.

Project Outline

I. Introduction [EW 1.1]

You can save a workbook, or a portion of a workbook, in two ways:

- A static (noninteractive) Web page is _____
  _____

- A dynamic (interactive) Web page includes _____
  _____

Publishing workbooks is _____

II. Saving an Excel workbook as a static Web page [EW 1.4]

HTML (hypertext markup language) is _____
_____

☞ To save an Excel workbook as a static Web page

1. _____
   _____

2. _____
   _____

3. _____

Click the Web Page Preview command to _____
_____

When you use the Save as Web Page command, a Save area displays in the Save As dialog box. In the Save area:

- The Entire Workbook option button indicates _____

  _____

- The Selection Sheet option button saves _____

  _____

- The Add interactivity check box saves _____

  _____

- The Publish button is _____

  _____

If you have access to a Web server:

- Click the Web Folders button to _____

- Under FTP locations you can _____

Round tripping is _____

A. Viewing the static Web page using your browser [EW 1.6]

☞ To view the static Web page using your browser

   1. _____

   2. _____

   3. _____

   4. _____

The static Web page is an ideal media for _____

III. Saving an Excel chart as a dynamic Web page [EW 1.7]

☞ To save an Excel chart as a dynamic Web page

   1. _____

      _____

   2. _____

      _____

   3. _____

      _____

      _____

   4. _____

In the Publish as Web Page dialog box, the Choose box allows _____

_____

A. Viewing and manipulating the dynamic Web page using your browser [EW 1.10]

☞ To view and manipulate the static Web page using your browser

   1. _____

2. _____

_____

3. _____

4. _____

The interactivity and functionality of a dynamic Web page allow you to _____

_____

B. Modifying the worksheet on a dynamic Web page [EW 1.11]

The Spreadsheet toolbar allows you to _____

_____

The Spreadsheet Property toolbox provides _____

_____

Modifying a dynamic Web page does not change _____

_____

Review

Matching (3)

Match each term on the left with the best description from the right.

___   1.   Web Page Preview command

___   2.   Publish button

___   3.   Spreadsheet toolbar

a.   allows you to invoke commonly used worksheet commands

b.   starts your browser and displays a static Web page

c.   allows you to save files to a Web folder

d.   saves the Web page to an FTP

e.   allows you to customize a Web page further

True/False (5)

*Circle **T** if the statement is true and **F** if the statement is false.*

T   F   1.   A dynamic Web page is similar to a printed report in that you can view it through your browser, but you cannot modify it.

T   F   2.   If you have access to a Web server, you can publish Web pages by saving them to a Web folder or to an FTP location.

T   F   3.   The Save As dialog box that displays when you use the Save as Web Page command is exactly the same as the dialog box that displays when you use the Save as command.

T   F   4.   Excel allows you to save an entire workbook, a sheet in the workbook, or a range on a sheet as a Web page.

T   F   5.   Modifying a dynamic Web page changes the makeup of the original workbook or the Web page stored on disk.

Fill in the Blanks (3)

Write a word (or words) in the blank to correctly complete each sentence.

1.   The Save as Web page command allows you to _____ workbooks, which is the process of making them available to others.

2.   The file format in which Excel saves a workbook as a Web page is called _____, which is a language browsers can interpret.

3.   Saving the Excel formats that allow an HTML file to be displayed in Excel is _____ the HTML file back to the application in which it was created.

Multiple Choice (2)

Circle the letter of the best answer.

1.   In the Save As dialog box that displays when you use the Save as Web page command, which of the following is selected by default?
   a.   the Add interactivity check box
   b.   the Selection Sheet option button
   c.   the Publish button
   d.   the Entire Workbook option button

2. What button on the Spreadsheet toolbar selects specific items you want to display in a list?
    a. AutoFilter
    b. Sort Ascending
    c. AutoSum
    d. Sort Descending

The Microsoft Internet Explorer Window (5)

Identify the indicated buttons on the Spreadsheet toolbar in Figure E7.

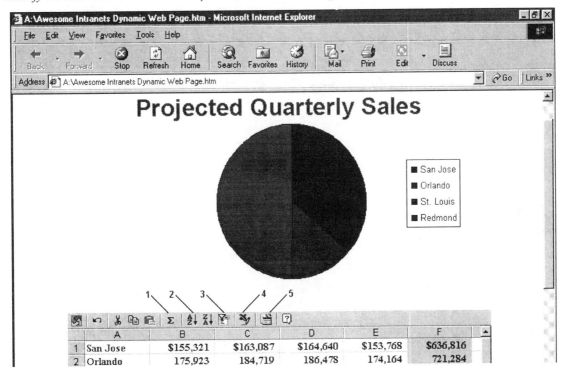

Figure E7

1. _____   4. _____

2. _____   5. _____

3. _____

Short Answer (2)

Write a brief answer to each question.

1. How is a static Web page different from a dynamic Web page? When would you use each type of Web page?

2. Why, after a workbook is saved as an HTML file, does the file continue to display in the Excel window as if it were saved as a Microsoft Excel workbook?

Activities

Use Help

Use Help to answer each question.

1. How do you **change data after you put it on a Web page**? Use the Index sheet to find out.

2. How can you **put Excel data on an existing Web page**? Use the Office Assistant to find out.

Expanding on the Lab

Perform the following tasks.

1. Start your browser. With the Data Disk in drive A, type a:\microprocessor plus dynamic web page.htm in the Address bar. When the Web page displays, print it.

2. Change cell B4 (January sales) to $904,327 and cell E4 (April sales) to $275,432.00. Total Sales (cell H4) should equal $3,275.875.00. The 3-D Pie Chart changes to reflect the new values. Print the Web page.

3. Click the Undo button on the Spreadsheet toolbar twice to return cell B4 and cell E4 to their original values.

4. Scroll down and change the values in the following cells: cell B15 (Base Salary) = 15%; cell B17 (Bonus) =15,000; and cell B20 (Payroll Tax) = 15.5%. Cell H12 (Total Payroll Expense) should equal $925,525.16. The 3-D Pie Chart changes to reflect the new values. Print the Web page.

5. Quit your browser. Compare the 3-D Pie Charts on the three printouts and note how they are different.

Microsoft Access 2000

Project One
Creating a Database Using
Design and Database Views

〰〰〰〰〰〰〰〰〰〰〰〰〰〰〰〰〰〰〰〰〰〰〰〰〰〰

Overview

In this project, you gain an understanding of database concepts by creating a database for Bavant Marine Services, a company performing routine boat maintenance and engine repairs for various marinas. After starting Access, you learn about the Database window and the Access desktop. You discover how to create tables, how to define data types, and how to determine the primary key for a table. Once the table is created, you find out how to add records to a table, correct errors in the data, and print the contents of a table. You learn how to create a form and to use both Datasheet view and Form view to view data. Using Report Wizard, you create a report for the Marina table. You also explore the features of Microsoft Access Help, including the Office Assistant. Finally, you investigate how to design databases to reduce redundancy.

Project Outline

I. What is Microsoft Access 2000? [A 1.6]

Microsoft Access 2000 is _____

_____

Key features of Access include:

- _____ • _____
- _____ • _____
- _____

II. Project One – Bavant Marine Services Database [A 1.6]

The term database describes _____

_____

- Records are _____
- A field contains _____

    A unique identifier or primary key is _____

A. Starting Access and creating a new database [A 1.9]

    ☞ To start Access

    1. _____

2. _____

_____

3. _____

4. _____

5. _____

_____

6. _____

_____

The Office Assistant is _____

7. _____

III. The Access desktop and the Database window [A 1.12]

- The title bar displays _____

The Close button is _____

- The menu bar contains _____

To open a menu _____

- The Database window toolbar contains _____

_____

An icon is _____

- The taskbar displays _____

- The status bar contains _____

The Database window is _____

_____

IV. Creating a table [A 1.13]

You describe the structure of a table by _____

For each field you indicate:

1. Field name _____

2. Data type _____

3. Description _____

You also must indicate which field or fields that make up the primary key for the table.

The data type indicates _____

Data types in this project:

1. Text _____

2. Number _____

3. Currency _____

☞ To create a table

    1. _____

    2. _____

    3. _____

A. Defining the fields [A 1.15]

A pane is a portion of the screen.

To move from the upper pane to the lower pane _____

The row selector is _____

☞ To define the fields in a table

    1. _____

    2. _____

       _____

    3. _____

       _____

    4. _____

       _____

    5. _____

       _____

    6. _____

B. Correcting errors in the structure [A 1.18]

   •   If you discover a mistake before pressing the TAB key _____

      _____

   •   If you accidentally add an extra field to the structure _____

      _____

   •   If you forget a field _____

      _____

   •   If you made the wrong field a primary key field _____

      _____

To start over _____

V. Saving a table [A 1.19]

Table names are _____

☞ To save a table

    1. _____

       _____

    2. _____

3. _____

VI. Adding records to a table [A 1.20]

In Datasheet view, the table is _____

☞ To add records to a table

1. _____

2. _____

The record selector is _____

3. _____

_____

4. _____

_____

5. _____

_____

6. _____

7. _____

VII. Closing a table and a database and quitting Access [A 1.24]

It is a good idea to close a table _____

☞ To close a table and database and quit Access

1. _____

2. _____

3. _____

VIII. Opening a database [A 1.25]

☞ To open a database

1. _____

2. _____

_____

3. _____

IX. Adding additional records [A 1.27]

Use the Navigation button to _____

_____

☞ To add additional records to a table

1. _____

2. _____

3. _____

4. _____

_____

5. _____

A. Correcting errors in the data [A 1.29]

- If you discover a mistake before pressing the TAB key _____

_____

- If you discover an incorrect entry later _____

_____

- If you add a record accidentally _____

_____

- If you cannot determine how to correct the data _____

_____

X. Previewing and printing the contents of a table [A 1.30]

Portrait orientation means _____

Landscape orientation means _____

Preview is _____

☞ To preview and print the contents of a table

1. _____

2. _____

3. _____

4. _____

5. _____

6. _____

Option button refers to _____

7. _____

8. _____

9. _____

_____

XI. Creating additional tables [A 1.34]

A database typically consist of more than one table.

☞ To create an additional table

1. _____

_____

_____

2. _____

_____

A. Adding records to the additional table [A 1.35]

☞ To add records to an additional table

1. _____

2. _____

3. _____

XII. Using a form to view data [A 1.36]

In Datasheet view, the data on the screen displays as a table.

In Form view, you see _____

A. Creating a form [A 1.37]

☞ To use the New Object: AutoForm button to create a form

1. _____

_____

2. _____

3. _____

B. Closing and saving a form [A 1.38]

☞ To close and save a form

1. _____

2. _____

3. _____

C. Opening the saved form [A 1.39]

☞ To open a form

1. _____

_____

2. _____

3. _____

D. Using the form [A 1.40]

You can use the form just as you used Datasheet view.

☞ To use a form

1. _____

E. Switching between Form view and Datasheet view [A 1.41]

☞ To switch from Form view to Datasheet view

1. _____

2. _____

3. _____

XIII. Creating a report [A 1.43]

A page header contains _____

The detail lines are _____

☞ To create a report

1. _____

_____

2. _____

3. _____

A. Selecting the fields for the report [A 1.44]

To indicate fields in the report, click the field in the Available Fields list.

☞ To select the fields for a report

1. _____

_____

2. _____

B. Completing the report [A 1.46]

☞ To compete a report

1. _____

_____

2. _____

3. _____

4. _____

5. _____

6. _____

C. Printing the report [A 1.48]

☞ To print a report

1. _____

_____

2. _____

XIV. Closing the database [A 1.49]

☞ To close a database

1. _____

XV.   Access Help system [A 1.49]

The Access Help system can be used to _____

A.   Using the Office Assistant [A 1.49]

The Office Assistant answers _____

IntelliSense™ technology, which is built into Access, understands _____

_____

☞   To obtain help using the Office Assistant

1. _____

_____

2. _____

3. _____

4. _____

XVI.   Designing a database [A 1.52]

Database design refers to _____

Redundancy means _____

Problems associated with redundancy:

1. _____

2. _____

3. _____

The solution to the problem is _____

This corrects the problems of redundancy in the following ways:

1. _____

2. _____

3. _____

Review

Matching (5)

Match each term on the right with the best description from the left.

___ 1. menu bar

___ 2. database window toolbar

___ 3. taskbar

___ 4. status bar

___ 5. title bar

a. displays various objects such as tables and reports in the database

b. displays the name of the product, Microsoft Access

c. displays names that represents lists of commands used to perform tasks in the database management system

d. displays different portions of a table in the Table window

e. displays the Start button, any active windows, and the current time

f. displays special information appropriate for the task

g. displays buttons that are used to perform tasks more quickly

True/False (10)

*Circle **T** if the statement is true and **F** if the statement is false.*

T   F   1. Microsoft Access is a powerful database management system (DBMS) that functions in the Windows environment and allows you to create and process data in a database.

T   F   2. In Access, all the tables, reports, forms, and queries created are stored in separate files.

T   F   3. Field names can contain periods and exclamation points (!) but not square brackets [ ].

T   F   4. Each field in a database table must have a unique name.

T   F   5. To create a table, right-click Create table in Design view and then click Print on the shortcut menu.

T   F   6. The row selector is a small box or bar that when clicked, selects the entire row.

T   F   7. To open a database table, right-click the table in the Database window and then click Open on the shortcut menu.

T   F   8. The advantage with Form view is that you can see multiple records at once.

T   F   9. When you use the Report Wizard, you select a field for a report by clicking the field in the Available Fields list box and then clicking the Add Field button.

T   F   10. Redundancy makes updating a database less difficult.

Definitions (5)

Briefly define each term.

1. shortcut menu _____

2. Database window _____

3. toolbar _____

4. row selector _____

5. ScreenTip _____

The Access Screen (5)

Identify the elements indicated in Figure A1.

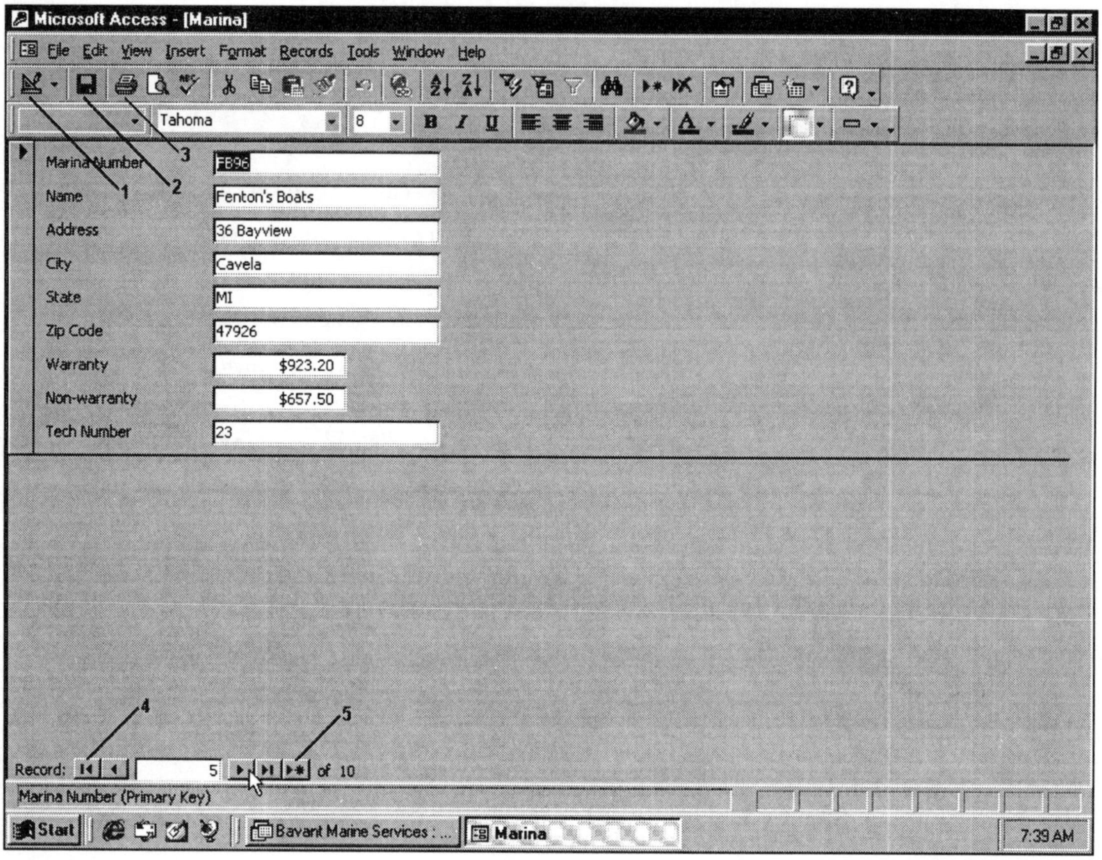

Figure A1

1. _____   4. _____

2. _____   5. _____

3. _____

Multiple Choice (5)

Circle the letter of the best answer.

1. What does a key symbol to the left of a field name mean?
   a. the field is the first field in the table
   b. values in the field can be used as passwords
   c. the field is the primary key for the table
   d. the field is the last field in the table

2. What is the small box called that when clicked selects an entire row?
   a. row highlighter
   b. record identifier
   c. record highlighter
   d. row selector

3. Which Navigation button moves past the last record in a table to a position for a new record?
   a. Add Record
   b. New Record
   c. Append Record
   d. Insert Record

4. How do you open a table in the Database window?
   a. right-click the table and then click Open on the shortcut menu
   b. right-click the table and then click Use on the shortcut menu
   c. left-click the table and then click Datasheet on the shortcut menu
   d. drag the table to the desktop

5. Which Navigation button moves you to the first record in a table?
   a. Start Record
   b. Top Record
   c. Beginning Record
   d. First Record

Dialog Box (5)

Answer the following questions about the Open Office Document dialog box shown in Figure A2.

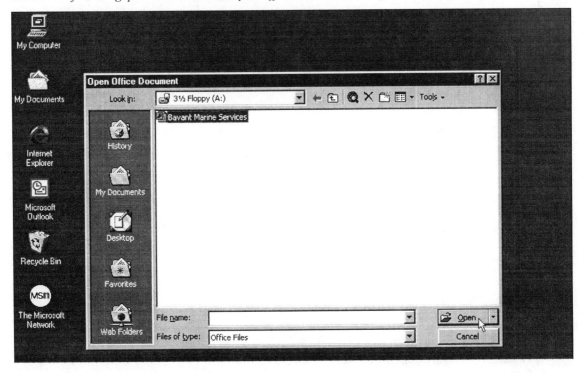

Figure A2

1. How was the dialog box displayed? _____

2. What existing database files are on drive A? _____

3. How would you find database files on drive C? _____

4. Which database file is currently selected? _____

5. How would you finish opening the database? _____

Fill in the Blanks (5)

Write a word (or words) in the blank to correctly complete each sentence.

1. The rows in a table are called _____ .

2. The columns in a table are called _____ .

3. If you must correct a record that is not on the screen, use the _____ buttons near the lower-left corner to move to the record.

4. If you discover a mistake before pressing the TAB key to move to the next field, you can correct it by first pressing the _____ key(s) and then typing the correct characters.

5. Each button on the toolbar contains a picture or _____ , depicting its function.

Sequence (5)

Use the numbers 1 – 5 to show the order in which these steps should be performed to obtain help using the Office Assistant.

____ Click the Search button.

____ Click the Close button on the Microsoft Access Help window title bar.

____ Type a word or phrase in the What would you like to do? text box.

____ Click Show Office Assistant on the Help menu.

____ Click the appropriate topic.

Short Answer (5)

Write a brief answer to each question.

1. When would you use landscape orientation? How do you switch to landscape orientation?

2. Why should you preview a report before you print it?

3. Why should you design a database to remove redundancy?

4. Why would you assign a data type of Text to the Zip Code field in the Client and Technician tables?

5. How does Form view differ from Datasheet view?

Activities

Use Help

Use Help to answer each question.

1. How do you **check the spelling of data** in Datasheet view? Use the Office Assistant to find out.

2. How can you **find specific occurrences of a value in a field** in Form view? Look in the Finding and Replacing Data book in the Finding and Sorting Data book on the Contents sheet to find out.

3. How do you open a **table** in the Database window? Use the Index sheet to find out.

Expanding on the Lab

Perform the following tasks.

1. Open the Sidewalk Scrapers database modified in Apply Your Knowledge 1.

2. Create a form for the Customer table.

3. Open the form and bring the record with Customer Number BH81 to the screen.

4. Change the address for BH81 (Laura Bond) to 520 Beard.

5. Switch to Datasheet view.

6. Print the table.

7. Change the address for Customer Number BH81 back to 407 Scott.

8. Close the table.

9. Click No when asked if you want to save the form.

Puzzle

Use the clues below to complete the word search puzzle. Words in the puzzle may be forward or backward, across, up and down, or diagonal.

Creating a Database

```
R  O  D  M  ■  ■  P  I  T  N  E  E  R  C  S
O  F  A  E  E  P  A  C  S  D  N  A  L  ■  Y
T  F  T  N  A  V  I  G  A  T  I  O  N  ■  E
C  I  A  U  ■  S  T  A  T  U  S  B  A  R  K
E  C  S  B  P  A  G  E  H  E  A  D  E  R  Y
L  E  H  A  ■  ■  R  A  B  E  L  T  I  T  R
E  A  E  R  R  E  D  U  N  D  A  N  C  Y  A
S  S  E  C  C  A  T  F  O  S  O  R  C  I  M
D  S  T  D  E  T  A  I  L  L  I  N  E  S  I
R  I  ■  R  O  W  S  E  L  E  C  T  O  R  R
O  S  I  N  T  E  L  L  I  S  E  N  S  E  P
C  T  E  P  Y  T  A  T  A  D  I  C  O  N  ■
E  A  W  E  I  V  M  R  O  F  I  E  L  D  ■
R  N  G  I  S  E  D  E  S  A  B  A  T  A  D
■  T  I  A  R  T  R  O  P  A  N  E  ■  ■  ■
```

Powerful database management system that functions in the Windows environment.

Collection of data organized in a manner that allows access, retrieval, and use of that data.

Rows in a database table.

Contains a specific piece of information within a record.

Field that serves as a unique identifier.

Positioned at the top of the Microsoft Access window.

Appears on the far right of the title bar.

Second bar in the Access Window, contains names that represent lists of commands.

Picture contained on each toolbar button, depicting its function.

Displays immediately above the windows taskbar with special information about the task on which you are working.

Indicates the kind of data that can be stored in a field.

Portion of the screen.

Small box that, when click, selects an entire row.

Description that displays when the mouse pointer rests on a toolbar button.

Represents a database table as a collection of rows and columns.

A collection of rows and columns.

Small box or bar to the left of a record.

Type of button found near the lower-left corner of the screen.

Type of orientation in which a printout is across the width of the page.

Type of orientation in which a printout is across the length of a page.

Displays a single record at a time.

Portion at the top of a report.

Lines printed for each report, containing only the fields specified in the order specified.

Answers questions and suggests more efficient ways to complete a task.

Type of technology that understands what you are trying to do and suggests better ways to do it.

The arrangement of data into tables and fields.

Storing the same fact in more than one place.

Microsoft Access 2000

Project Two
Querying a Database Using
the Select Query Window

~~~~~~

Overview

In this project, you learn to query a database using Access. You learn how to create and run queries, use wildcards, and enter conditions using comparison operators. You also create queries using AND criterion and OR criterion. In some of the queries, you join tables. Finally, you learn how to use calculated fields and statistics as well as how to save a query.

Project Outline

    I. Introduction [A 2.4]

        A query is _____

    II. Project Two – Querying the Bavant Marine Sales Database [A 2.4]

        A. Opening the database [A 2.6]

          ☞ To open a database

            1. _____

            2. _____

            3. _____

    III. Creating a new query [A 2.6]

        A Select Query window is _____

        As a standard practice, maximize the Select Query window as soon as you have created it.

        ☞ To create a query

          1. _____

                _____

          2. _____

          3. _____

          4. _____

                _____

        The design grid is _____

5. _____

_____

6. _____

A. Using the Select Query window [A 2.9]

You create a query by _____

B. Displaying selected fields in a query [A 2.9]

Only fields that appear in the design grid will be included in the query results.

To display certain fields _____

To remove a field _____

☞ To include fields in the design grid

1. _____

_____

2. _____

3. _____

_____

C. Running a query [A 2.11]

☞ To run a query

1. _____

2. _____

D. Printing the results of a query [A 2.12]

☞ To print the results of a query

1. _____

2. _____

E. Returning to Design view [A 2.12]

☞ To return to Design view

1. _____

2. _____

3. _____

F. Closing a query [A 2.14]

☞ To close a query

1. _____

2. _____

IV. Including all fields in a query [A 2.14]

Select the asterisk (*) to indicate _____

☞   To include all fields in a query

    1. _____

       _____

    2. _____

    3. _____

    4. _____

V.   Clearing the design grid [A 2.16]

Clear the query to _____

☞   To clear the query

    1. _____

    2. _____

VI.   Entering criteria [A 2.17]

When you use queries, usually you are looking for _____

A.   Using text data in criteria [A 2.17]

Text data is _____

☞   To use text data in a criterion

    1. _____

       _____

    2. _____

    3. _____

B.   Using wildcards [A 2.18]

Wildcards are _____

• The asterisk (*) represents _____

• The question mark (?) represents _____

☞   To use a wildcard

    1. _____

       _____

    2. _____

C.   Criteria for a field not in the result [A 2.19]

Occasionally, you may need to enter criteria that should not appear in the query results.

☞   To use criteria for a field not included in the results

    1. _____

    2. _____

    3. _____

    4. _____

D. Using numeric data in criteria [A 2.21]

To enter a number in a criterion _____

☞ To use a number in a criterion

   1. _____

   2. _____

   3. _____

E. Using comparison operators [A 2.22]

Unless otherwise specified, Access assumes the criteria entered involve _____

Comparison operators:

>   _____   >= _____

<   _____   <= _____

NOT _____

☞ To use a comparison operator in a criterion

   1. _____

   2. _____

   3. _____

VII. Using compound criteria [A 2.23]

Compound criterion are _____

• In AND criterion _____

• An OR criterion _____

A. Using AND criteria [A 2.23]

To combine criteria with AND _____

☞ To use a compound criterion involving AND

   1. _____

       _____

   2. _____

B. Using OR criteria [A 2.25]

To combine criteria with OR _____

☞ To use a compound criterion involving OR

   1. _____

   2. _____

       _____

   3. _____

VIII.   Sorting data in a query [A 2.26]

You sort records to _____

The sort key is _____

- The major sort key (primary sort key) is _____

- The minor sort key (secondary sort key) is _____

☞ To sort data in a query

1.   _____

2.   _____

3.   _____

4.   _____

A.   Sorting on multiple keys [A 2.27]

☞ To sort on multiple keys

1.   _____

2.   _____

_____

3.   _____

The major sort key *must* appear _____

B.   Omitting duplicates [A 2.29]

☞ To omit duplicates

1.   _____

2.   _____

_____

3.   _____

4.   _____

_____

IX.   Joining tables [A 2.31]

You join tables to _____

A join line is _____

☞ To join tables

1.   _____

2.   _____

3.   _____

4.   _____

_____

5.   _____

A. Restricting records in a join [A 2.34]

Sometimes, you will not want to include all possible records when you join tables.

☞ To restrict the records in a join

1. _____

_____

2. _____

X. Using calculated fields in a query [A 2.35]

A calculated field is _____

To include calculated fields in queries, you enter _____

_____

Computations can include addition (+), subtraction (-), multiplication (*), and division (/). You also can include parentheses to indicate which computations should be done first.

☞ To use a calculated field in a query

1. _____

2. _____

3. _____

_____

4. _____

5. _____

XI. Calculating statistics [A 2.38]

Microsoft Access supports the built-in statistics: COUNT, SUM, AVG (average), MAX (largest value), MIN (smallest vale), STDEV (standard deviation), VAR (variance), FIRST, and LAST.

☞ To calculate statistics

1. _____

2. _____

3. _____

_____

4. _____

5. _____

6. _____

A. Using criteria in calculating statistics [A 2.40]

☞ To use criteria in calculating statistics

1. _____

2. _____

_____

    3. _____

    4. _____

B. Grouping [A 2.41]

Grouping means _____

☞ To use grouping

    1. _____

    2. _____

    3. _____

XII. Saving a query [A 2.42]

In many cases, you will construct a query you will want to run again.

☞ To save a query

    1. _____

    2. _____

Once you have saved a query, you can use it at any time in the future by opening it.

The query is run against _____

XIII. Closing a database [A 2.43]

☞ To close a database

    1. _____

Review

Matching (5)

Match each term on the left with the best description from the right.

____ 1. design grid

____ 2. text data

____ 3. comparison operator

____ 4. sort key

____ 5. join line

a. field on which the records are ordered in a particular way

b. drawn between matching fields indicating two tables are related

c. the area where you specify fields to be included in a query

d. symbol that indicates that all fields are to be included in a query

e. creating groups of records that share some characteristic

f. entries in a field whose type is any characters

g. used if you want something other than an exact match

True/False (10)

*Circle **T** if the statement is true and **F** if the statement is false.*

T F 1. The Select Query window contains a design grid, which is the area where you specify fields to include in the query, sort order, and criteria.

T F 2. The most widespread of all the query languages is a language called Delphi.

T F 3. If you wanted to sort the results of a query by city within state, city would be the major sort key and state would be the minor sort key.

T F 4. When you include a computed field in a query, you must use the Zoom dialog box to enter the formula for the field.

T F 5. One of the key features that distinguishes database management systems from file management systems is the ability to join tables.

T F 6. In OR criterion, each individual criterion must be true in order for the compound criterion to be true.

T F 7. To enter a number in a criterion, type the number without any dollar signs or commas.

T F 8. If a field is included in the design grid, it must display in the results.

T F 9. The set of records that make up the answer to a query display in Form view.

T F 10. To clear out the entries in the design gird, close the Select Query window without saving the query or click the Clear Grid command on the Edit menu.

Definitions (5)

Briefly define each term.

1. query _____

2. wildcards _____

3. sort _____

4. join _____

5. grouping _____

The Access Screen (5)

Identify the elements indicated in Figure A3.

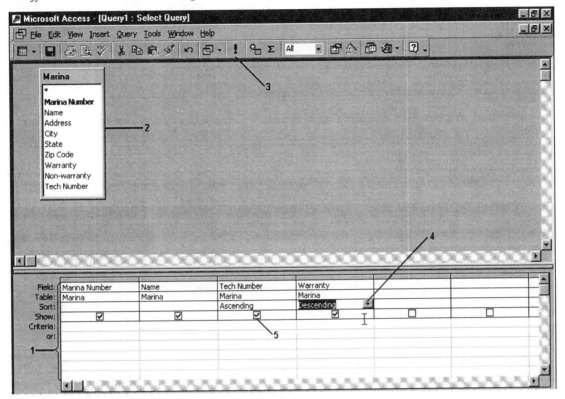

Figure A3

1. _____   4. _____

2. _____   5. _____

3. _____

Multiple Choice (5)

Circle the letter of the best answer.

1. How can you include all fields in a query without having to select each field individually?
   a. double-click the asterisk (*) in the field list box
   b. leave the first column of the design grid blank
   c. type the word ALL in the first column of the design grid
   d. double-click the word ALL in the field list box

2. What wildcard represents any individual character?
   a. the asterisk (*)
   b. the exclamation point (!)
   c. the ampersand (&)
   d. the question mark (?)

3. Why would you place two criteria on the same line in the design grid?
   a. to specify sorting
   b. to specify AND criterion
   c. to specify grouping
   d. to specify OR criterion

4. If you want to sort by warranty amount within technician number, how must the fields be placed in the design grid?
    a. the Warranty field to the left of the Tech Number field
    b. the Warranty field above the Tech Number field
    c. the Tech Number field to the left of the Warranty field
    d. the Tech Number field above the Warranty field

5. What statistic allows you to find the smallest value in a field?
    a. SMALL
    b. LOW
    c. MIN
    d. LEAST

Dialog Box (5)

Answer the following questions about the Zoom dialog box shown in Figure A4.

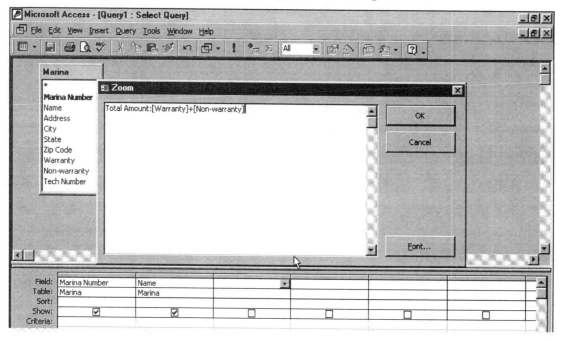

Figure A4

1. How was the dialog box displayed? _____

2. What mathematical operation is being performed? _____

3. What is the name of the calculated field? _____

4. What fields from the table are included in the expression? _____

5. When the OK button is clicked, where will a portion of the expression display? _____

Fill in the Blanks (5)

Write a word (or words) in the blank to complete each sentence correctly.

1. You create a query by making entries in a special window called a(n) _____.

2. The _____ wildcard represents any collection of characters.

3. If you are sorting on more than one field, the more important field is called the _____.

4. A(n) _____ is a field that can be computed by performing operations (addition, subtraction, multiplication, or division) on other fields.

5. COUNT, SUM, and AVG are some of the built-in _____ that Microsoft Access supports.

Sequence (5)

Use the numbers 1 – 5 to show the order in which these steps should be performed to use criteria for a field not included in the results.

____   Type the criteria for the field not included in the results.

____   Click the View button to return to Design view. On the Edit menu, click Clear Grid.

____   Run the query by clicking the Run button.

____   In the design grid, include the fields in the query.

____   Click the Show check box for the field not to be included in the results.

Short Answer (5)

Write a brief answer to each question.

1. Why would you want to save a query?

2. When would you double-click the asterisk (*) in the field list on the Select Query window?

3. When do you need to include the Total row in the design grid?

4. How do you omit duplicates when you sort data?

5. When do you use the Zoom dialog box?

Activities

Use Help

Use Help to answer each question.

1. How do you **insert or delete a criteria row in a query**? Look in the Using Criteria and Expressions to Retrieve Data book in the Working with Queries book on the Contents sheet to find out.

2. How can you **retrieve records that don't contain values using a query**? Use the Office Assistant to find out.

3. What is a **parameter query** and when would you use one? Use the Index sheet to find out.

Expanding on the Lab

Perform the following tasks.

1. Open the Sidewalk Scrapers database from the Access folder on the data disk.

2. Create a new query for the Customer table.

3. Display and print the Customer Number, Name, and Address fields of all customers who have an address on Secord.

4. Clear the design grid.

5. Display and print the average balance grouped by Worker Id.

6. Close the query without saving it.

7. Create a new query for the Worker table.

8. Display and print the Worker Id, First Name, Last Name, and Weekly Pay (Pay Rate *40) of all workers.

9. Close the query without saving it. Close the Sidewalk Scrapers database.

Puzzle
Use the clues given to complete the crossword puzzle.

Querying a Database

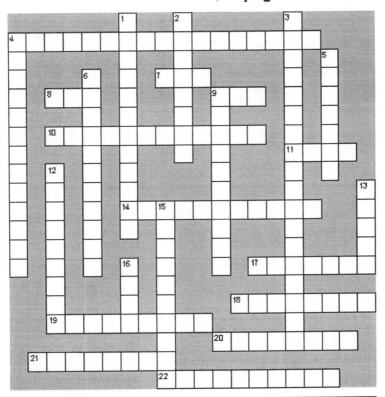

Down

1. Requires that each individual criterion be true for the compound criterion to be true.
2. Creating collections of records that share some common characteristics.
3. Entered if you want something other than an exact match.
4. Dispose of entries in the design grid so you can start over.
5. When sorting, type of sort key that is more important.
6. Window in which a query is created by making entries.
9. COUNT, SUM, AVG, MAX, MIN, STDEV, VAR, FIRST, and LAST.
12. Symbols that represent any character or combination of characters.
13. A question represented in a way that Access can understand.
15. Type of field that can be calculated from other fields.
16. Find records in two tables that have identical values in matching fields.

Across

4. Used when the data for which you are searching must satisfy more than one condition.
7. Query Design toolbar button clicked to initiate a query.
8. Query language in which users ask questions by filling in a table on the screen.
9. The most widespread of all query languages.
10. Wildcard symbol that represents any individual character.
11. Order the records in answer to a query in a particular way.
14. Makes a compound criterion true provided that either individual criterion is true.
17. Field on which records are arranged.
18. Data in a field whose type is text.
19. When sorting, type of sort key that is less important.
20. Select in the field list to indicate that all fields are to be included.
21. Drawn by Access between matching fields in two tables.
22. Area where you specify fields to be included in a query.

Microsoft Access 2000
Project Three
Maintaining a Database Using the Design and Update Features of Access

Overview

This project covers the issues involved in maintaining a database. You learn how to use Form view to add a record. You learn how to locate and filter records. You change and delete records. You also learn how to change the structure of a table, create validation rules, and specify referential integrity by creating relationships. You make mass changes using update queries. Finally, you learn how to create indexes to improve performance.

Project Outline

I. Introduction [A 3.4]

Maintaining the database means _____

Updating can include:

- Mass updates allow _____

- Mass deletions allow _____

Periodically, maintenance can involve the need to restructure the database; that is _____

_____

Indexes are _____

II. Project Three – Maintaining the Bavant Marine Services Database [A 3.5]

III. Opening the database [A 3.6]

☞ To open a database

1. _____

2. _____

3. _____

IV. Adding, changing, and deleting records in a table [A 3.6]

A. Adding records [A 3.6]

In Form view you use _____

You also can use Form view to update the data in a table.

☞ To use a form to add records

1. _____

2. _____

3. _____

4. _____

5. _____

_____

6. _____

B. Searching for a record [A 3.8]

Searching means _____

The function of the Find button is _____

☞ To search for a record

1. _____

_____

_____

2. _____

3. _____

To find the next record that satisfies a criterion, repeat the process.

C. Changing the contents of a record [A 3.10]

Insert mode means _____

Overtype mode means that the characters typed will replace the existing characters.

To switch between Insert and Overtype modes, press _____

☞ To update the contents of a field

1. _____

2. _____

D. Switching between views [A 3.11]

Sometimes, after working in Form view, it would be helpful to see several records at a time.

☞ To switch from Form view to Datasheet view

1. _____

2. _____

3. _____

E. Filtering records [A 3.12]

To have only the record or records that satisfy a criterion display, use a filter.

Filter by selection is _____

☞ To filter records

1. _____

2. _____

☞ To remove a filter

1. _____

2. _____

F. Deleting records [A 3.14]

Delete the records (remove them) from a table when _____

☞ To delete a record

1. _____

_____

2. _____

3. _____

V. Changing the structure of a database [A 3.15]

When you create a database, you define its structure.

A database's structure indicates _____

The structure may have to be changed because _____

_____

A. Changing the size of a field [A 3.15]

☞ To change the size of a field

1. _____

2. _____

3. _____

4. _____

B. Adding a new field [A 3.17]

For a variety of reasons, tables frequently need to be expanded to include additional fields.

☞ To add a field to a table

1. _____

2. _____

3. _____

_____

4. _____

5. _____

C. Deleting a field from a table [A 3.19]

To delete a field that no longer is needed, open the table in Design view, click the row

selector for the field to select it, and then press _____

D. Updating the restructured database [A 3.19]

Changes to the structure of a table are available immediately.

If the record to be changed is not on the screen, use _____

If the field to be changed is not on the screen, use _____

☞ To update the contents of a field

1. _____

_____

2. _____

_____

E. Resizing columns [A 3.20]

Resizing the column is done to _____

The field selector is _____

☞ To resize a column

1. _____

2. _____

3. _____

4. _____

_____

5. _____

6. _____

F. Using an update query [A 3.23]

An update query is _____

The Update To: row of an update query indicates _____

☞ To use an update query to update all records

1. _____

2. _____

3. _____

_____

_____

4. _____

_____

5. _____

6. _____

G. Using a delete query to delete a group of records [A 3.26]

A delete query is _____

☞ To use a delete query to delete a group of records

1. _____

   _____

2. _____

   _____

3. _____

4. _____

VI. Creating validation rules [A 3.28]

Validation rules are_____

Validation text is _____

Validation rules can indicate a required field, establish a range of values, and specify a default value.

- A required field is _____

- A range of values is_____

- A default value is_____

A. Specifying a required field [A 3.28]

☞ To specify a required field

1. _____

   _____

2. _____

B. Specifying a range [A 3.29]

☞ To specify a range

1. _____

   _____

   _____

C. Specifying a default value [A 3.30]

☞ To specify a default value

1. _____

   _____

D. Specifying a collection of legal values [A 3.31]

Legal values are legitimate entries for a field, according to the validation rules.

☞ To specify a collection of legal values

1. _____

   _____

   _____

E. Using a format [A 3.32]

A format is _____

A format symbol is _____

- The format symbol > causes _____

- The format symbol < causes _____

☞ To specify a format

1. _____

_____

F. Saving rules, values, and formats [A 3.33]

☞ To save the validation rules, default values, and formats

1. _____

2. _____

3. _____

G. Updating a table that contains validation rules [A 3.34]

When updating a table that contains validation rules, Access _____

_____

_____

To leave a field or close a table after entering data that violates a validation rule _____

_____

_____

H. Making individual changes to a field [A 3.36]

☞ To make individual changes

1. _____

2. _____

_____

3. _____

VII. Specifying referential integrity [A 3.38]

Referential integrity is _____

A foreign key is _____

To specify referential integrity, you must define a relationship between the tables by using the

Relationships command. The type of relationship specified is called a one-to-many relationship.

A one-to-many relationship means _____

_____

_____

☞ To specify referential integrity

1. _____

2. _____

3. _____

_____

4. _____

5. _____

6. _____

A relationship line is _____

7. _____

When a relationship is specified, attempts to add a record whose field does not match or to delete a record for whom related records exist will result in an error message.

VIII. Using subdatasheets [A 3.41]

A subdatasheet displays _____

☞ To use a subdatasheet

1. _____

_____

2. _____

3. _____

IX. Ordering records [A 3.42]

To change the order in which records display _____

☞ To use the Sort Ascending button to order records

1. _____

_____

2. _____

A. Ordering records on multiple fields [A 3.43]

To sort data that displays on multiple fields, the major and minor keys must be _____

_____

When the major and minor keys are in position, select both fields. To select the fields, click the field selector for the first field (major key) and then _____

_____

A field selector is_____

☞ To use the Sort Ascending button to order records on multiple fields

   1. _____

     _____

     _____

   2. _____

X. Creating and using indexes [A 3.44]

An index is _____

The index key is _____

Benefits of an index are: _____

_____

Sorting is _____

A. How does Access use an index? [A 3.46]

Access uses an index to _____

_____

B. When should you create an index? [A 3.47]

Disadvantages of an index are: _____

_____

Create an index on a field if:

   1. _____

   2. _____

   3. _____

   4. _____

C. Creating single-field indexes [A 3.47]

A single-field index is _____

☞ To create a single-field index

   1. _____

     _____

   2. _____

   3. _____

D. Creating multiple-field indexes [A 3.48]

Multiple-field indexes are _____

The Indexes button is _____

☞ To create a multiple-field index

   1. _____

2. _____

_____

3. _____

_____

4. _____

_____

XI. Closing the database [A 3.50]

☞ To close a database

1. _____

Review

Matching (5)

Match each term on the left with the best description from the right.

___ 1. field selector

___ 2. validation rule

___ 3. validation text

___ 4. required field

___ 5. default value

a. convention that the data entered by a user must follow

b. displayed in a particular field before the user adds a record

c. field in one table whose values are required to match the primary key of another table

d. small bar at the top of a column that is clicked to select a field

e. message displayed if a user violates a validation rule

f. query that will delete all the records satisfying the criteria entered in the query

g. field in which the user actually must enter data

True/False (10)

*Circle **T** if the statement is true and **F** if the statement is false.*

T   F   1. Updating can include mass updates or mass deletions.

T   F   2. In Form view, you can display the first record in a table by clicking the Top Record button.

T   F   3. To decrease the size of a column, position the mouse pointer on the right boundary of the column's field selector and drag the line to the right.

T   F   4. The property that the value in a foreign key must match another table's primary key is called entity integrity.

T   F   5. In the relationships window, the relationship line displays an infinity symbol (∞) to indicate the *many* table.

T   F   6. Access automatically uses any indexes that you create.

T   F   7. A single-field index is an index whose key is a single field.

T   F   8. If you request that Access locate a particular record and Access determines that there is no index available, it will create the necessary index automatically.

T   F   9. To force all letters in a field to display as lowercase, use the asterisk (*) symbol in the Format text box.

T   F   10. If you resize a column in Datasheet view, Access prompts you to save changes to the layout of the table when you close the Datasheet window.

Definitions (5)

Briefly define each term.

1. update query _____

2. format symbol _____

3. referential integrity _____

4. foreign key_____

5. multiple-field indexes _____

The Access Screen (5)

Identify the elements indicated in Figure A5.

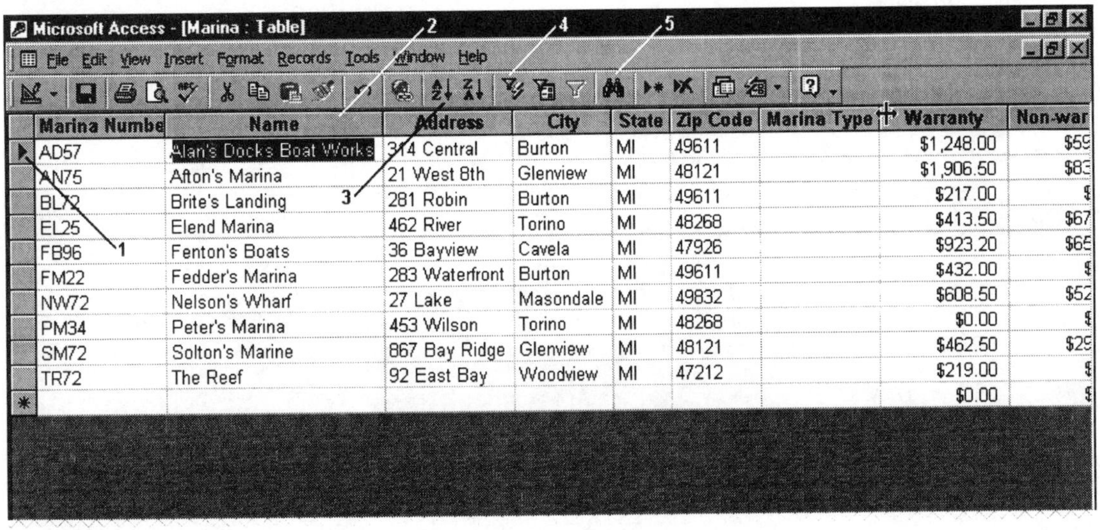

Marina Numbe	Name	Address	City	State	Zip Code	Marina Type	Warranty	Non-war
AD57	Alan's Docks Boat Works	314 Central	Burton	MI	49611		$1,248.00	$59
AN75	Afton's Marina	21 West 8th	Glenview	MI	48121		$1,906.50	$83
BL72	Brite's Landing	281 Robin	Burton	MI	49611		$217.00	$
EL25	Elend Marina	462 River	Torino	MI	48268		$413.50	$67
FB96	Fenton's Boats	36 Bayview	Cavela	MI	47926		$923.20	$65
FM22	Fedder's Marina	283 Waterfront	Burton	MI	49611		$432.00	$
NW72	Nelson's Wharf	27 Lake	Masondale	MI	49832		$608.50	$52
PM34	Peter's Marina	453 Wilson	Torino	MI	48268		$0.00	$
SM72	Solton's Marine	867 Bay Ridge	Glenview	MI	48121		$462.50	$29
TR72	The Reef	92 East Bay	Woodview	MI	47212		$219.00	$
							$0.00	$

Figure A5

1. ______________________
2. ______________________
3. ______________________
4. ______________________
5. ______________________

Multiple Choice (5)

Circle the letter of the best answer.

1. How do you move to the first record in a table in Form view?
   a. click the Top Record button
   b. click the First Record button
   c. press the HOME key
   d. press the PAGE UP key

2. Which format symbol causes Access to convert uppercase letters automatically to lowercase?
   a. >
   b. /
   c. ~
   d. <

3. Which condition should be entered in the Validation Rule text box to ensure that entries in a currency field are between $0.00 and $500.00?
   a. >$0 and <$500
   b. >0 and <500
   c. >=$0.00 and <=$500.00
   d. >=0 and <=500

4. If the letters OVR display on the status bar, what does it mean?
   a. Access is in Insert mode
   b. Access is in Find mode
   c. Access is in Update mode
   d. Access is in Overtype mode

5. To order records on two fields, what must you press as you click the field selector for the second field?
   a. the ALT key
   b. the SHIFT key
   c. the CTRL key
   d. the DOWN arrow

Dialog Box (5)

Answer the following questions about the Edit Relationships dialog box shown in Figure A6.

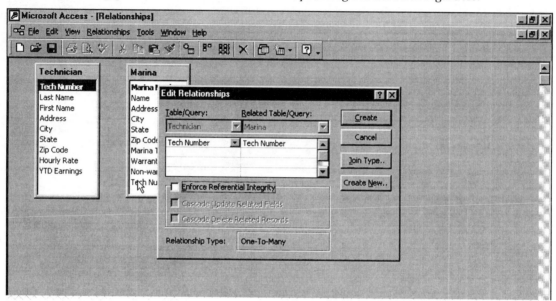

Figure A6

1. How was the dialog box displayed? _____

2. Which table is the *one* table in the relationship? _____

3. Which table is the *many* table in the relationship? _____

4. What fields are used to relate the tables? _____

5. What is the purpose of the Enforce Referential Integrity check box? _____
   _____

Fill in the Blanks (5)

Write a word (or words) in the blank to complete each sentence correctly.

1. In the database environment _____ means looking for records that satisfy some criteria.

2. When you create a database, you define its _____; that is, you indicate the names, types, and sizes of all fields.

3. You can use a(n) _____ to affect the way data is displayed in a field.

4. The fact that a(n) _____ is available is indicated by a plus symbol that displays in front of the rows in a table.

5. Physically rearranging records in a different order, which is called _____, can be a very time-consuming process.

Sequence (5)

Use the numbers 1 – 5 to show the order in which these steps should be performed to create a single-field index.

____   Click Design on the shortcut menu. If necessary, maximize the window.

____   Click the Indexed text box in the Field Properties pane. Click the Indexed text box down arrow.

____   In the Database window, right-click the table.

____   Click the row selector to select the field for the index key.

____   Click Yes (Duplicates OK).

Short Answer (5)

Write a brief answer to each question.

1. What is a one-to-many relationship? How does Access visually depict the relationship in the Relationships window?

2. When should you create an index?

3. How does using an index to order records differ from sorting records?

4. How is Overtype mode different from Insert mode? How do you switch between Overtype mode and Insert mode?

5. If you specify referential integrity between two tables, what types of updates will Access prohibit?

Activities

Use Help

Use Help to answer each question.

1.   What is the maximum length of the **Validation Text property setting**? Use the Index sheet to find out.

2.   How do you **find a record by its record number in Datasheet or Form view**? Look in the Finding and Replacing Data book in the Finding and Sorting Data book on the Contents sheet to find out.

3.   How do you **delete an index**? Use the Office Assistant to find out.

Expanding on the Lab

Perform the following tasks.

1.   Open the Sidewalk Scrapers database. Open the Worker table in Design view.

2.   Make the Last Name field a required field.

3.   Specify a default value of $4.00 for the Pay Rate field.

4.   Specify that any value entered in the Pay Rate field must be greater than or equal to $4.00 and less than or equal to $7.00.

5.   Create an index on the Last Name field.

6.   Format the Last Name field so any lowercase letters display in uppercase. Save the changes to the Worker table.

7.   Open the Worker table in Datasheet view.

8.   Sort the data in descending order by Pay Rate.

9.   Print the table in landscape orientation.

Puzzle

The terms described by the phrases below are written below each line in code. Break the code by writing the correct term above the coded word. Then, use your broken code to translate the final sentences.

1. Modifying the data in a database to keep it up to date.

   UYTDQYTDTDH

2. Looking for records that satisfy some criteria.

   KSYEANTDH

3. The simplest type of filter.

   BTOQSE GX KSOSAQTJD

4. Defined when a database initially is created.

   KQEWAQWES

5. Small bar at the top of a column that you click to select the entire field in a datasheet.

   BTSOM KSOSAQJE

6. Used to change records as a group.

   WPMYQS VWSEX

7. Used to remove records as a group.

   MSOSQS VWSEX

8. Regulations that the data entered by a user must follow.

   XYOTMYQTJD EWOSK

9. Where the user actually must enter data.

   ESVWTESM BTSOM

10. Certain limits that validation rules can make sure a user's entry lies.

    EYDHS JB XYOWSK

11. Displayed on the screen in a particular field before the user begins adding a record.

    MSBYWOQ XYOWS

12. Affects the way data is displayed in a field.

    BJEUYQ

13. Property that ensures the value in a foreign key must match that of another table's primary key.

    ESBSESDQTYO TDQSHETQX

14. Field in one table whose values are required to match the primary key of another table.

    BJESTHD ISX

15. Type of relationship between two tables specified in the Relationship command.

    JDS-QJ-UYDX

16. Visually displays the fields used to connect tables.

    ESOYQTJDKNTP OTDS

17. Indicated by a plus symbol that displays in front of the rows in a table.

    KWGMYQYKNSSQ

18. Feature that speeds up searching and sorting in a table based on key values.

    TDMSF

19. Physically rearranging records in a different order.

    KJEQTDH

20. Type of index whose key is a combination of fields.

UWOQTPOS-BTSOM

YKI CSSXSK (ZZZ.YKICSSXSK.AJU) TK Y AYESBWOOX UYTDQYTDSM MYQYGYKS

QNYQ AJUPYESK DSZ VWSKQTJDK QJ QYGOSK JB QNJKS YOESYMX YKISM, YDM

PJTDQK WKSEK QJ QNS ZSG KTQS UJKQ OTISOX QJ PEJXTMS YD YDKZSE.

Microsoft Access 2000

Web Feature
Publishing to the Internet
Using Data Access Pages

~~~~~~

Overview

In this Web feature, you learn how to create a data access page to enable users to access the data in a database via the Internet. You work with the Page Wizard to create such a page. The data access page then is previewed from within Access. Finally, you see how to use the data access page.

Project Outline

I. Introduction [AW 1.1]

Microsoft Access 2000 supports data access pages.

A data access page is _____

_____

An HTML (hypertext markup language) document can be _____

Data pages can be run only in _____

To use a data access page on the Internet, the page and the database must be located on a server.

A server is _____

II. Opening the database [AW 1.3]

☞ To open a database

1. _____

2. _____

3. _____

III. Creating a data access page [AW 1.3]

☞ To create a data access page

1. _____

2. _____

3. _____

4. _____

_____

5. _____

6. _____

_____

7. _____

8. _____

_____

9. _____

_____

IV. Previewing the data access page [AW 1.8]

☞ To preview the data access page

1. _____

2. _____

3. _____

_____

V. Using the data access page [AW 1.9]

To use the data access page _____

_____

On the record navigation toolbar:

- Click the Sort Ascending button to ensure _____

- Use the navigation buttons just as _____

- Click the Help button to display _____

In the Microsoft Access Data Pages Help window:

- Clicking the plus symbol (+)in front of a category will change _____

_____

- Clicking the question mark symbol (?) in front of a topic will display _____

_____

Review

Matching (3)

Match each term on the left with the best description from the right.

___ 1. plus symbol (+)   a. indicates Help window topic details

___ 2. minus symbol (-)   b. indicates Help window topics expanded

___ 3. question mark   c. indicates Help window topics available on the Web
         symbol (?)
                                   d. indicates Help window topics not expanded

                                   e. indicates no Help window topics available

True/False (5)

*Circle **T** if the statement is true and **F** if the statement is false.*

T   F   1. The fact that a data access page is bound directly to a database means that it can access data
             in the database directly.

T   F   2. You cannot use a data access page to change the contents of existing records, to delete
             records, or to add new records.

T   F   3. In order to use a data access page on the Internet, both the page and the database would
             need to be located on a server that would be available to the Internet.

T   F   4. While in Access, you can preview what a data access page will look like in a browser by
             using Web Page Preview on the shortcut menu.

T   F   5. To use a data access page, start Access, type the location of the page, and then press the
             HOME key.

Fill in the Blanks (3)

Write a word (or words) in the blank to correctly complete each sentence.

1. A(n) _____ is an HTML document that can be bound directly to data in the database.

2. The fact that a data access page is a(n) _____ means that it can be run on the Internet.

3. A(n) _____ is a computer that shares its resources with other computers on the Internet.

Multiple Choice (2)

Circle the letter of the best answer.

1. Data access pages created in Access can be run in what browser?
    a. Netscape Navigator
    b. Microsoft Internet Explorer
    c. Mosaic
    d. all of the above

2. To create a data access page, what would you select in the New Data Access Page box?
    a. Design View
    b. Existing Web page
    c. Page Wizard
    d. AutoPage: Columnar

Dialog Box (5)

Answer the following questions about the Page Wizard dialog box shown in Figure A7.

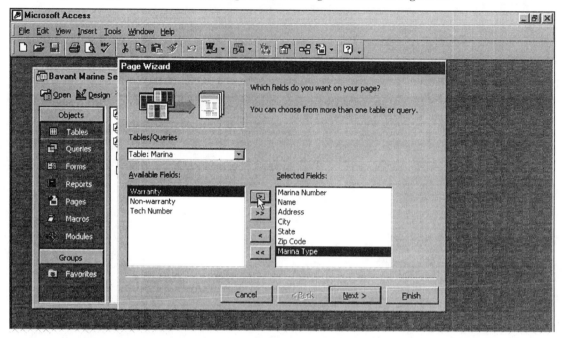

Figure A7

1. What fields have been selected? _____

2. What fields still are available? _____

3. The fields are from what table? _____

4. To what button is the mouse pointer pointing? _____

5. How would you move to the subsequent Page Wizard dialog box? _____

Short Answer (2)

Write a brief answer to each question.

1. For what purposes can a data access page be used?

2. How can you determine what a newly created data access page will look like in the browser?

Activities

Use Help

Use Help to answer each question.

1. How do you **follow a hyperlink on a data access page**? Using the Microsoft Access Data Pages Help window, look in the Working with Hyperlinks book in the Working with Data Access Pages book to find out.

2. How do you **print a data access page**? Using the Microsoft Access Data Pages Help window, look in the Working with Data book in the Working with Data Access Pages book to find out.

Expanding on the Lab

Perform the following tasks.

1. Start Internet Explorer and then open the Worker data access page.

2. Use the data access page to change Chris Carter's telephone number to 555-7461 and Elena Sanchez's hourly pay rate to $5.00.

3. Use the data access page to add a classmate to the Worker table. Use 98 as the worker id number and $6.50 as the hourly rate.

4. Use the data access page to add your instructor to the Worker table. Use 01 as the worker id number and an appropriate amount as the hourly pay rate.

5. Quit Internet Explorer and then start Access. Open the Worker table in Datasheet view. You should have 6 records. Print the table and then quit Access.

6. Start Internet Explorer and then open the Worker data access page. Delete the record you added for your classmate and the record you added for your instructor. Change Chris Carter's telephone number to 555-7641 and Elena Sanchez's hourly pay rate to $4.75.

7. Quit Internet Explorer.

Microsoft PowerPoint 2000
Project One
Using a Design Template and AutoLayouts
to Create a Presentation

Overview

This project illustrates starting PowerPoint and creating a multi-level bulleted list presentation. You learn about PowerPoint design templates, objects, and attributes. First, you create an introduction to a presentation by changing the text font style to italic and increasing font size on the title slide. Upon completing these tasks, you save your presentation. Then, you create three multi-level bulleted list slides to explain how to study effectively in college. Next, you learn how to view the presentation in slide show view, how to quit PowerPoint, and how to open an existing presentation. You use the Spelling checker to search for spelling errors and learn how the Office Assistant Style checker identifies inconsistencies in design specifications. Using the slide master, you adjust the Before paragraph line spacing on every slide to make better use of white space. You learn how to display the presentation in black and white. Then, you learn how to print hard copies of your slides to make overhead transparencies. Finally, you learn how to use the PowerPoint Help system.

Project Outline

I. What is Microsoft PowerPoint 2000? [PP 1.6]

Microsoft PowerPoint 2000 is _____

A PowerPoint presentation also is called a(n) _____

Eight PowerPoint features simplify creating presentations:

- Word processing allows _____
- Outlining allows _____
- Charting allows _____
- Drawing allows _____
- Inserting multimedia adds _____
- Web support allows_____
- E-mailing allows _____
- Using Wizards allows _____

The AutoContent Wizard gives_____

The Pack and Go Wizard helps you to _____

The PowerPoint Viewer allows you to _____

II.   Project One – Effective Study Skills [PP 1.8]

A bullet is _____

A bulleted list is _____

III.   Starting a presentation as a new Office document [PP 1.10]

The Start button on the taskbar is the quickest way to _____

The Start menu displays _____

Use the New Office Document command to _____

☞   To start a new presentation

1.   _____

2.   _____

3.   _____

4.   _____

The taskbar button area displays _____

The active application is _____

A slide is _____

Objects are _____

The title slide is _____

IV.   The PowerPoint window [PP 1.12]

A default setting is _____

Attributes are _____

Slide layouts:

•   Landscape orientation _____

•   Portrait orientation _____

When you start PowerPoint, the default slide layout is _____

A.   PowerPoint views [PP 1.13]

A view is _____

•   Slide view displays _____

•   Outline view displays _____

•   Slide show view displays _____

•   Normal view displays _____

•   Slide sorter view displays _____

To change views, click _____

Normal view displays 3 panes: _____

After you have created at least two slides, scroll bars, scroll arrows, and scroll boxes can be used to _____

B. Placeholders, title area, object area, mouse pointer, and scroll bars [PP 1.13]

　1. Placeholders [PP 1.14]

　　Placeholders are _____

　　A text placeholder displays _____

　　You place graphic elements in _____

　　_____

　　An objects is _____

　　• An unfilled object is _____

　　• A filled object is _____

　　• A text object is _____

　2. Title Area [PP 1.14]

　　The Title Area is _____

　3. Object Area [PP 1.14]

　　The Object Area is _____

　4. Mouse pointer [PP 1.14]

　　The mouse pointer can _____

　5. Scroll bars [PP 1.14]

　　• The vertical scroll bars display _____

　　• The horizontal scroll bar displays _____

C. Menu bar, Standard toolbar, Formatting toolbar, Drawing toolbar, and status bar [PP 1.14]

　1. Menu bar [PP 1.14]

　　The menu bar displays _____

　　To display a menu _____

　　When you point to a command with an arrow _____

　　A short menu lists _____

　　A full menu shows _____

　　• To display a full menu _____

　　Hidden commands are _____

　　Dimmed commands indicate _____

　2. Standard, Formatting, and Drawing toolbars [PP 1.15]

　　A ScreenTip displays _____

　　The Standard toolbar contains _____

　　The Formatting toolbar contains _____

　　By default, the Standard and Formatting toolbars are on the same row. To display the

　　entire Standard toolbar, _____

　　The Drawing toolbar contains _____

3. Status bar [PP 1.17]

The status bar consists of _____

A shortcut menu contains _____

D. Resetting menus and toolbars [PP 1.17]

☞ To reset my usage data and toolbar buttons [MO C.1]

1. _____

2. _____

_____

3. _____

_____

4. _____

_____

5. _____

E. Displaying the Formatting toolbar in its entirety [PP 1.17]

☞ To display the Formatting toolbar in its entirety

1. _____

2. _____

V. Choosing a design template [PP 1.18]

A design template provides _____

☞ To choose a design template

1. _____

2. _____

3. _____

4. _____

VI. Creating a title slide [PP 1.20]

With the exception of a blank slide, PowerPoint assumes _____

A. Entering the presentation title [PP 1.20]

☞ To enter the presentation title

1. _____

2. _____

The insertion point is _____

A paragraph is _____

PowerPoint line wraps text that _____

A selection rectangle is _____

The AutoFit Text feature _____

B. Correcting a mistake when typing [PP 1.22]

Use the BACKSPACE key to _____

Clicking the Undo button allows you to _____

_____

Clicking the Redo button reverses _____

C. Entering the presentation subtitle [PP 1.22]

☞ To enter the presentation subtitle

1. _____

2. _____

VII. Text attributes [PP 1.24]

A text attribute is _____

Design Template Text Attributes	
ATTRIBUTE	**DESCRIPTION**
Color	_____ _____
Font	_____
Font size	_____ _____
Font style	_____ _____
Subscript	_____ _____
Superscript	_____ _____

A. Changing the font size [PP 1.24]

Font size is measured in points. A point is 1/72 of an inch in height.

☞ To increase font size

1. _____

2. _____

3. _____

A ScreenTip contains _____

The Font Size box indicates _____

4. _____

When you click the Font Size box arrow _____

5. _____

You can use the Increase Font Size button to _____

You can use the Decrease Font Size button to _____

B. Changing the style of text to italic [PP 1.27]

☞ To change the text font style to italic

1. _____

The Italic button is _____

2. _____

VIII. Saving the presentation on a floppy disk [PP 1.28]

☞ To save a presentation on a floppy disk

1. _____

2. _____

3. _____

4. _____

5. _____

The .ppt extension stands for _____

IX. Adding a new slide to a presentation [PP 1.31]

☞ To add a new slide using the Bulleted List AutoLayout

1. _____

2. _____

3. _____

X. Creating a bulleted list slide [PP 1.33]

A multi-level bulleted list slide is_____

A level is _____

• A demoted paragraph is _____

Click the Demote button to _____

• A promoted paragraph is_____

Click the Promote button to _____

A. Entering a slide title [PP 1.34]

☞ To enter a slide title

1. _____

B. Selecting an Object Area placeholder [PP 1.35]

☞ To select an Object Area placeholder

1. _____

C. Typing a multi-level bulleted list [PP 1.36]

☞ To type a multi-level bulleted list

1. _____

2. _____

3. _____

4. _____

5. _____

☞ To type the remaining text for Slide 2

1. _____

2. _____

XI. Adding new slides with the same AutoLayout [PP 1.40]

☞ To add a new slide with the same AutoLayout

1. _____

☞ To complete Slide 3

1. _____

2. _____

3. _____

4. _____

5. _____

6. _____

7. _____

8. _____

☞ To create Slide 4

1. _____

2. _____

3. _____

4. _____

5. _____

6. _____

7. _____

8. _____

9. _____

XII.   Ending a slide show with a black slide [PP 1.42]

☞ To end a slide show with a black slide

1. _____

2. _____

3. _____

XIII. Saving a presentation with the same file name [PP 1.44]

☞ To save a presentation with the same file name

1. _____

2. _____

XIV.   Moving to another slide in normal view [PP 1.44]

In the slide pane, you can click the Previous Slide or Next Slide buttons to _____

_____

A slide's Zoom setting affects _____

When you drag the scroll box, the slide indicator displays _____

A.   Using the scroll box on the slide pane to move to another slide [PP 1.44]

☞ To use the scroll box on the slide pane to move to another slide

1. _____

2. _____

3. _____

XV.   Viewing the presentation using slide show [PP 1.46]

The Slide Show button allows you to _____

A.   Starting slide show view [PP 1.46]

☞ To start slide show view

1. _____

2. _____

B.   Advancing through a slide show manually [PP 1.47]

☞ To move manually through slides in a slide show

1. _____

2. _____

C.   Using the Popup menu to go to a specific slide [PP 1.48]

To display the slide show view Popup menu _____

Popup menu commands:

• The Next command moves _____

• The Previous command moves_____

• The Go command jumps _____

- The Slide Navigator dialog box contains _____
- The End Show command exits _____
☞ To display the Popup menu and go to a specific slide
    1. _____
    2. _____
    3. _____

D. Using the Popup menu to end a slide show [PP 1.50]

The End show command is used to _____

☞ To use the Popup menu to end a slide show
    1. _____
    2. _____
    3. _____

XVI. Quitting PowerPoint [PP 1.50]

☞ To quit PowerPoint
    1. _____
    2. _____

XVII. Opening a presentation [PP 1.51]

The Open Office Document command is used to _____

A. Opening an existing presentation [PP 1.51]

☞ To open an existing presentation
    1. _____
    2. _____
    3. _____

XVIII. Checking a presentation for spelling and consistency [PP 1.54]

A. Checking a presentation for spelling errors [PP 1.54]

A custom dictionary is available for _____

When a word displays in the Spelling dialog box, you can:

- Ignore _____
- Ignore all _____
- Select _____
- Change _____
- Add _____
- View _____
- Add the spelling error to _____

B. Starting the Spelling checker [PP 1.54]

☞ To start the Spelling checker

1. _____

2. _____

3. _____

4. _____

C. Checking a presentation for style consistency [PP 1.56]

Office Assistant tips can range from _____

_____

XIX. Correcting errors [PP 1.57]

A. Types of corrections made to presentations [PP 1.57]

• Additions are _____

• Deletions are _____

• Replacements are _____

B. Deleting text [PP 1.57]

Three methods to delete text are:

• _____

• _____

• _____

C. Replacing text in an existing slide [PP 1.57]

You can replace text by _____

XX. Changing line spacing [PP 1.57]

A component's master is_____

The title master is _____

The slide master is _____

A. Displaying the slide master [PP 1.58]

☞ To display the slide master

1. _____

2. _____

B. Changing line spacing on the slide master [PP 1.59]

When you click the line space command _____

☞ To change line spacing on the slide master

1. _____

2. _____

3. _____

4. _____

5. _____

6. _____

XXI. Displaying a presentation in black and white [PP 1.63]

The Grayscale Preview button allows _____

☞ To display a presentation in black and white

1. _____

2. _____

3. _____

4. _____

XXII. Printing a presentation [PP 1.64]

A hard copy, or printout, is _____

A rough draft is _____

A. Saving a presentation before printing [PP 1.64]

☞ To save a presentation before printing

1. _____

2. _____

B. Printing the presentation [PP 1.65]

☞ To print the presentation

1. _____

2. _____

C. Making a transparency [PP 1.67]

You can make overhead transparencies using _____

_____

XXIII. PowerPoint Help System [PP 1.67]

You use the PowerPoint Help system to _____

A. Using the Office Assistant [PP 1.67]

The Office Assistant _____

IntelliSense technology _____

☞ To obtain Help using the Office Assistant:

1. _____

2. _____

3. _____

4. _____

PowerPoint Help System		
TYPE	*DESCRIPTION*	*HOW TO ACTIVATE*
Answer Wizard		
Contents sheet		
Detect and Repair		
Hardware and Software Information		
Index sheet		
Office Assistant		
Office on the Web		
Question Mark button and What's This? command		

XIV.   Quitting PowerPoint [PP 1.69]

☞   To quit PowerPoint:

1. _____

2. _____

Review

Matching (5)

Match each term on the left with the best description from the right.

____ 1. Object Area

____ 2. Drawing toolbar

____ 3. Standard toolbar

____ 4. Formatting toolbar

____ 5. shortcut menu

a. collection of tools for drawing and editing objects

b. contains tools for changing text attributes, such as font

c. collection of placeholders for the title, text, and clip art

d. contains tools to execute the more common commands found on the menu bar and for setting Zoom

e. the location of the text placeholder where you will type the main heading of a new slide

f. the empty area on a slide that can contain placeholders for displaying subtitles, clip art, or charts

g. used to move forward or backward through a presentation

True/False (10)

*Circle **T** if the statement is true and **F** if the statement is false.*

T   F   1. The Line Spacing dialog box contains four boxes: Between lines, Above lines, Below lines, and After paragraphs.

T   F   2. The Style Checker Options dialog box has two tabbed sheets: Case and End Punctuation, and Visual Clarity.

T   F   3. PowerPoint inserts text to the right of the insertion point.

T   F   4. The slide master controls the appearance of the title slide, whereas the title master controls the appearance of the other slides in a presentation.

T   F   5. When a word is added to the AutoCorrect list during a spelling check, any future misspelling of the word is corrected automatically as you type.

T   F   6. The Slide Navigator dialog box is displayed after clicking the Go command in the slide show view shortcut menu known as the Popup menu.

T   F   7. When you drag the Slide Show button at the lower-left corner of the PowerPoint window, the slide indicator displays the number and the title of the slide you are about to display.

T   F   8. The indent and outdent buttons on the Formatting toolbar allow you to type a multi-level bulleted list.

T   F   9. The Bulleted List AutoLayout is one of the 30 different AutoLayouts available in PowerPoint.

T   F   10. A superscript character displays or prints above and immediately to one side of another character.

Definitions (5)

Briefly define each term.

1. text attribute_____

2. title master _____

3.   custom dictionary _____

4.   active application_____

5.   line wrap_____

The PowerPoint Screen (5)

Identify the elements indicated in Figure PP1.

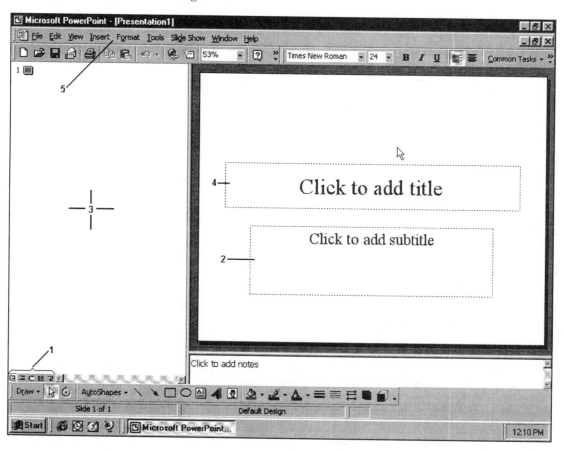

Figure PP1

1. _____   4. _____

2. _____   5. _____

3. _____

Multiple Choice (5)

Circle the letter of the best answer.

1.   Which text attributes can you change with tools found on the Formatting toolbar?
     a.   font
     b.   font size
     c.   alignment
     d.   all of the above

2. Which action is performed when a word displays in the Spelling dialog box?
   a. the letters appear in bold type
   b. the letters are italicized
   c. the word is added to the custom dictionary if you click the Add button
   d. suggested spellings display in the Corrections box

3. What is the name of the blinking vertical line indicating where the next character will display?
   a. typing spot
   b. insertion point
   c. I-beam
   d. letter locator

4. What happens if you click the printer icon in the tray status area on the taskbar during the printing process?
   a. the printing process is cancelled
   b. two copies of the presentation print
   c. you are allowed to delete files in the queue
   d. the presentation is saved on a floppy disk

5. If you click the Grayscale Preview button before you print your presentation, what appearance will the slide background have?
   a. black
   b. hidden
   c. grayscale
   d. white

Dialog Box (5)

Answer the following questions about the Line Spacing dialog box shown in Figure PP2.

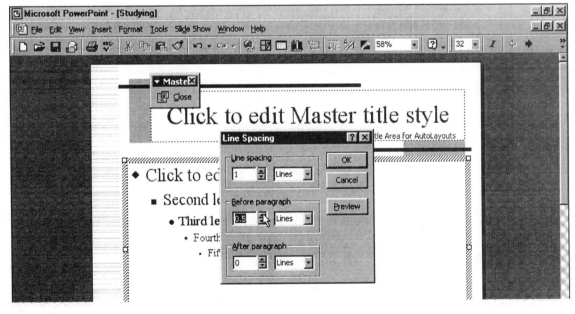

Figure PP2

1. How was the dialog box displayed?_____

2. What unit of measure is shown in the list boxes? _____

3. How much line spacing will appear within the paragraph? _____

4. How much line spacing will appear before each paragraph? _____

5. How would you display the line spacing changes without making them permanent? _____

Fill in the Blanks (5)

Write a word (or words) in the blank to complete each sentence correctly.

1. The first printing of your presentation, called the _____, allows you to proofread the slide show to check for errors and readability.

2. PowerPoint automatically appends the extension _____ to a file name.

3. When you drag the _____ on the vertical scroll bar, the slide indicator displays the number and title of the slide you are about to display.

4. Use the _____ command to open an existing presentation from a floppy disk.

5. The _____ automatically checks for case and end punctuation consistency and for visual clarity.

Sequence (5)

Use the numbers 1 – 5 to show the order in which these steps should be performed to choose a design template.

____   The selected slide displays with the new design template applied.

____   Click the Apply button.

____   Click Apply Design Template to open the Apply Design Template dialog box.

____   Scroll through the list of design templates to the desired template.

____   Click the Common Tasks menu button on the Formatting toolbar.

Short Answer (5)

Write a brief answer to each question.

1. What is the difference between text that is line wrapped and text that is AutoFit?

2. What are the three methods to delete unwanted text? When would you use each of these methods?

3. How does the title master differ from the slide master? How do they control the appearance of your presentations?

4. Why should you save a presentation frequently as you are creating it? How does saving a new document differ from saving an existing document?

5. How does a PowerPoint object change when it displays in black and white? When would you want your presentation to display in black and white?

Activities

Use Help

Use Help to answer each question.

1. How do you **add a button to a toolbar**? Use the Office Assistant to find out.

2. How do you **change text color**? Look in the Adding and Formatting Text book on the Contents sheet to find out.

3. How do you **insert a symbol** in your PowerPoint slide? Use the Index sheet to find out.

Expanding on the Lab

Perform the following tasks.

1. Open the Money Freedom presentation created in In the Lab 1.

2. Change the title of Slide 1 to Making the Most of Your Money and change the font size to 30.

3. In Slide 2, add Use a money market mutual fund as a third Second level paragraph under Have an emergency money fund.

4. In Slide 3, change the First level bulleted paragraph, Make a budget and stick to it, to Stick to the budget you create for yourself.

5. In Slide 4, add Investigate 401K plans offered by your employer as a fourth First level bulleted paragraph.

6. Check the spelling of your presentation.

7. Display the revised presentation in black and white.

8. Print the revised black and white presentation.

9. Quit PowerPoint without saving the revised presentation.

Puzzle

Write the word described by each clue in the puzzle below. Words can be written forward or backward, across, up and down, or diagonally. The first letter of each word already appears in the puzzle.

P											
		P									F
									C		
						S	💻				
		💻	T		B						
	P			O	P						B
		H	N		E	H					P
	C				I		Q				
	💻				I		💻	B	N		
A									💻		
		S	B						T		
P						T			A		

Complete presentation graphics program.

One of 24 available that has placeholders for various objects.

PowerPoint document.

Checker that helps identify errors in your presentation.

A symbol; usually a dot that precedes text.

Defines the appearance and shape of text.

Attribute button on Formatting toolbar that tilts text sideways.

Attributes are characteristics such as font, font size, font style, or color.

Office Document command on the Start menu that retrieves an existing presentation.

Segment of text with same format that begins when you press the ENTER key and ends when you press the ENTER key again.

Button that returns you to the previous screen.

Tool on Standard toolbar that starts a blank presentation.

Types include title, menu, status, and scroll.

Design that provides consistency by determining the color scheme, font and font size, and layout of a presentation.

Type of copy that is a printed copy of presentation.

PowerPoint file name extension.

Empty objects on a new slide surrounded by a dashed line.

Basic unit of a PowerPoint presentation.

Menu that displays when you right-click a slide in slide show view.

Tool on Standard toolbar that deletes text.

Online assistance.

In Spelling dialog box, opens the custom dictionary, adds the word, and continues checking rest of presentation.

Types include dialog and scroll.

Button on title bar that ends PowerPoint and returns control to desktop.

Command that displays the subsequent slide.

Sheet in Help System used when you know the term about which you are seeking Help.

Microsoft PowerPoint 2000

Project Two
Using Outline View and Clip Art
to Create a Slide Show

Overview

This project illustrates the use of outline view, clip art, and animation effects. You create a slide presentation in outline view where you enter all the text in the form of an outline. You arrange the text using the Promote and Demote buttons. Once your outline is complete, you change slide layouts and add clip art to the Object Area placeholders. After adding clip art to another slide without using a clip art region in the Object Area placeholder, you move and size the picture. You add slide transition effects and text animation effects. Then you apply animation effects to clip art. You learn how to run an animated slide show demonstrating slide transition and animation effects. Finally, you print the presentation outline and slides using the Print command on the File menu and e-mail the presentation.

Project Outline

I. Creating a presentation from an outline [PP 2.4]

When you build a presentation, PowerPoint automatically creates five views. They are _____

_____

When creating a presentation in outline view, the first step is to type a title.

The outline title is_____

II. Project Two – Searching for Scholarships [PP 2.5]

III. Starting a new presentation [PP 2.6]

☞ To start a new presentation

1. _____
2. _____
3. _____
4. _____
5. _____
6. _____
7. _____

IV. Using outline view [PP 2.7]

Outline view provides _____

An outline is _____

PowerPoint limits the number of heading levels to six:

- Heading level 1 is _____
- Heading level 2 is _____
- Heading level 3 is _____
- Heading level 4 is _____
- Heading level 5 is _____
- Heading level 6 is _____

☞ To change the view to outline view and display the Outline toolbar

1. _____

2. _____

3. _____

4. _____

PowerPoint can produce slides from an outline created with a word processor, if you save the

outline as _____

The file extension RTF stands for _____

A. The PowerPoint window in outline view [PP 2.10]

When the PowerPoint window is in outline view, the Outlining toolbar displays.

Buttons on the Outlining Toolbar	
BUTTON NAME	*DESCRIPTION*
Promote	_____
Demote	_____
Move Up	_____
Move Down	_____
Collapse	_____
Expand	_____
Collapse All	_____
Expand All	_____
Summary Slide	_____

Buttons on the Outlining Toolbar	
BUTTON NAME	*DESCRIPTION*
Show Formatting	_____
More Buttons	_____

V. Creating a presentation in outline view [PP 2.10]

When you drag and drop slide text or individual slides _____

A. Creating a title slide in outline view [PP 2.11]

☞ To create a title slide in outline view

1. _____

2. _____

3. _____

VI. Adding a slide in outline view [PP 2.12]

☞ To add a slide in outline view

1. _____

2. _____

VII. Creating multi-level bulleted list slides in outline view [PP 2.13]

An informational slide _____

☞ To create a multi-level bulleted list slide in outline view

1. _____

_____

2. _____

_____

3. _____

_____

A. Creating subordinate slides [PP 2.15]

Subordinate slides are _____

☞ To create a subordinate slide

1. _____

2. _____

3. _____

4. _____

5. _____

6. _____

7. _____

8. _____

B. Creating a second subordinate slide [PP 2.16]

☞ To create a second subordinate slide

1. _____

2. _____

3. _____

4. _____

C. Creating a third subordinate slide [PP 2.17]

☞ To create a third subordinate slide

1. _____

2. _____

3. _____

4. _____

5. _____

VIII. Creating a closing slide in outline view [PP 2.18]

A closing slide _____

Closing slides are used to:

• _____

• _____

• _____

• _____

• _____

☞ To create a closing slide in outline view

1. _____

2. _____

3. _____

4. _____

5. _____

6. _____

7. _____

IX. Saving a presentation [PP 2.19]

☞ To save a presentation

1. _____

2. _____

3. _____

X. Reviewing a presentation in slide sorter view [PP 2.20]

   ☞ To change the view to slide sorter view

1. _____

   ☞ To change the view to slide view

1. _____

2. _____

XI. Changing slide layout [PP 2.22]

After creating a slide, you can change its layout by clicking the Common Tasks button on the

Formatting toolbar and then clicking _____

The Slide Layout dialog box allows you to _____

   ☞ To change slide layout to Clip Art & Text

1. _____

2. _____

3. _____

XII. Adding clip art to a slide [PP 2.24]

Clip art offers _____

Microsoft Clip Gallery 5.0 is _____

A. Inserting clip art into an Object Area placeholder [PP 2.24]

   ☞ To insert clip art into an Object Area placeholder

1. _____

2. _____

3. _____

4. _____

5. _____

B. Inserting clip art on other slides [PP 2.27]

A bulletin board system is _____

   ☞ To change the slide layout to Text & Clip Art and insert clip art

1. _____

2. _____

3. _____

4. _____

5. _____

6. _____

☞ To change the slide layout to Clip Art & Text and insert clip art

1. _____

2. _____

3. _____

4. _____

5. _____

6. _____

C. Inserting clip art on a slide without a clip art region [PP 2.30]

☞ To insert clip art on a slide without a clip art region

1. _____

2. _____

3. _____

4. _____

5. _____

6. _____

XIII. Moving clip art [PP 2.31]

☞ To move clip art

1. _____

2. _____

XIV. Changing the size of clip art [PP 2.32]

Use the Format Picture command to _____

The Size sheet contains _____

Aspect ratio is_____

When the Lock aspect ratio check box displays a check mark _____

☞ To change the size of clip art

1. _____

2. _____

3. _____

4. _____

A. Creating a hyperlink [PP 2.35]

The AutoFormat as you type option changes _____

_____

A hyperlink is _____

_____

☞   To create a hyperlink

    1. _____

    2. _____

    3. _____

B.   Saving the presentation again [PP 2.35]

☞   To save a presentation

    1. _____

A default setting in PowerPoint allows for fast saves, which _____

_____

If you want to full save a copy of the complete presentation, click _____

_____

XV.   Adding a header and footer to outline pages [PP 2.35]

•   A header displays _____

•   A footer displays _____

A.   Using the Notes and Handouts sheet to add headers and footers [PP 2.36]

☞   To use the Notes and Handouts sheet to add headers and footers

    1. _____

    2. _____

    3. _____

    4. _____

XVI.   Adding animation effects [PP 2.37]

Slide transition effects are used to _____

Custom animation effects define _____

A.   Slide Sorter toolbar [PP 2.37]

The Slide Sorter toolbar displays when you are in slide sorter view.

Buttons and Boxes on the Slide Sorter Toolbar	
BUTTON NAME	FUNCTION
Slide Transition	_____
Slide Transition Effects	_____
Animation Effects	_____
Animation Preview	_____
Hide Slide	_____

Buttons and Boxes on the Slide Sorter Toolbar	
BUTTON NAME	*FUNCTION*
Rehearse Timings	_____
Summary Slide	_____
Speaker Notes	_____
Common Tasks	_____
More Buttons	_____

B. Adding slide transitions to a slide show [PP 2.38]

The SHIFT+click technique is used to _____

☞ To add slide transitions to a slide show

1. _____

2. _____

3. _____

4. _____

5. _____

6. _____

XVII. Applying animation effects to bulleted slides [PP 2.42]

☞ To use the slide master to apply animation effects to all bulleted slides

1. _____

2. _____

3. _____

4. _____

5. _____

6. _____

7. _____

8. _____

9. _____

XVIII. Animating clip art objects [PP 2.46]

A. Displaying a slide in slide view [PP 2.46]

☞ To display a slide in slide view

1. _____

    B. Animating clip art [PP 2.46]

       ☞ To animate clip art

         1. _____

         2. _____

XIX. Formatting and animating a title slide [PP 2.47]

       ☞ To change text font style to italic and increase font size

         1. _____

         2. _____

         3. _____

         4. _____

       ☞ To animate text

         1. _____

         2. _____

         3. _____

         4. _____

         5. _____

    A. Saving the presentation again [PP 2.49]

       ☞ To save a presentation on a floppy disk

         1. _____

XX. Running an animated slide show [PP 2.49]

       ☞ To run an animated slide show

         1. _____

         2. _____

         3. _____

         4. _____

XXI. Printing in outline view [PP 2.51]

    A. Printing an outline [PP 2.51]

       ☞ To print an outline

         1. _____

         2. _____

         3. _____

         4. _____

         5. _____

         6. _____

If the Collapse All button on the Outlining toolbar is recessed _____

If the Expand All button on the Outlining toolbar is clicked _____

B. Printing presentation slides [PP 2.54]

☞ To print presentation slides

1. _____

2. _____

3. _____

4. _____

5. _____

XXII. E-mailing a slide show from within PowerPoint [PP 2.55]

☞ To e-mail a slide show from within PowerPoint

1. _____

2. _____

3. _____

4. _____

A. Saving and quitting PowerPoint [PP 2.57]

☞ To save changes and quit PowerPoint

1. _____

2. _____

Review

Matching (5)

Match each term on the left with the best description from the right.

___ 1. Promote button

___ 2. Demote button

___ 3. Move Up button

___ 4. Move Down button

___ 5. Collapse button

a. indents or moves a selected paragraph down one level, to the right

b. hides all heading levels except the title of the selected slide

c. changes position with the paragraph located above the selected paragraph

d. displays all heading levels and text for the selected slide

e. creates a bulleted list slide from the titles of the selected slides

f. outdents or moves a selected paragraph up one level, to the left

g. changes position with the paragraph located below the selected paragraph

True/False (10)

*Circle **T** if the statement is true and **F** if the statement is false.*

T F 1. An outline will print as last viewed in outline view.

T F 2. PowerPoint has more than 100 custom animation effects.

T F 3. To remove a slide transition effect when displaying the presentation in slide sorter view, select Delete Effects in the Slide Transition Effect box.

T F 4. The ALT+click technique is used to select more than one slide.

T F 5. When you click the Print button on the Standard toolbar, PowerPoint prints a hard copy of the presentation component last selected in the Print what box in the Print dialog box.

T F 6. Custom animation effects define animation, sound effects, and timing for objects on a slide.

T F 7. A fast save saves only the changes made since the last time the presentation was saved.

T F 8. Aspect ratio is the relationship between title text and clip art.

T F 9. Demoting a paragraph indents or moves it to the left.

T F 10. A monitor's aspect ratio is determined by the number of pixels displaying per unit of measurement, such as a centimeter or an inch.

Definitions (5)

Briefly define each term.

1. outline view _____

2. Slide Layout dialog box _____

3. slide sorter view _____

4. outline _____

5. informational slide _____

The PowerPoint Screen (5)

Identify the elements indicated in Figure PP3.

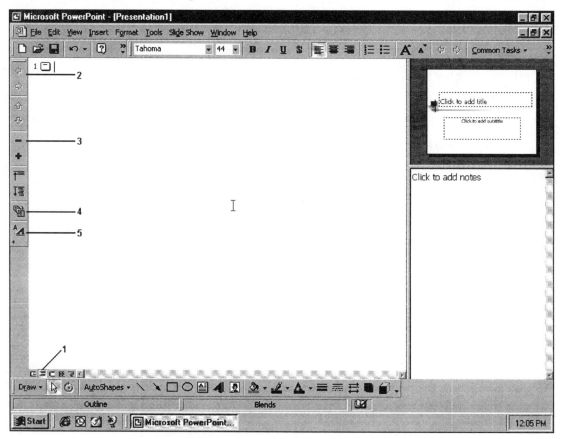

Figure PP3

1. _____
2. _____
3. _____

4. _____
5. _____

Multiple Choice (5)

Circle the letter of the best answer.

1. What does the file extension RTF stand for?
   a. Restored Text Format
   b. Resolution To Format
   c. Replacement Text Font
   d. Rich Text Format

2. Files saved with what format can be imported directly into your presentation?
   a. PCT
   b. JPG
   c. WPG
   d. PCD

3. Which button hides all heading levels except the title of the selected slide?
   a. Expand All
   b. Promote
   c. Collapse
   d. Expand

4. What is the function of a subordinate slide?
   a. to gracefully end a presentation
   b. to introduce the subject of the presentation
   c. to use indentation to establish a hierarchy
   d. to support the main topic

5. When you add a new slide in normal view, to what layout does PowerPoint default?
   a. Text & Clip Art
   b. Clip Art & Text
   c. Object Area
   d. Bulleted List AutoLayout

Dialog Box (5)

Answer the following questions about the Format Picture dialog box shown in Figure PP4.

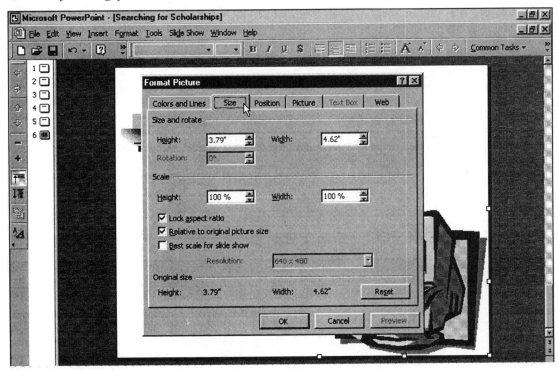

Figure PP4

1. How was the dialog box displayed?_____

2. What can you change the size of by using this dialog box? _____

3. What is an aspect ratio?_____

4. Which area of the tab on the dialog box shown can you use to enter a picture's height and width as a percentage of the object's original size?_____

5. What is the significance of the check in the Lock aspect ratio check box?_____
   _____

Fill in the Blanks (5)

Write a word (or words) in the blank to complete each sentence correctly.

1. A PowerPoint outline is created in _____ view.

2. The _____ button moves the selected paragraph up one level in the outline hierarchy.

3. A(n) _____ system allows users to communicate with each other and to share files.

4. The _____ technique allows you to select more than one slide.

5. PowerPoint allows up to _____ heading levels.

Sequence (5)

Use the numbers 1 – 5 to show the order in which these steps should be performed to insert clip art into an Object Area placeholder.

____   Press the ENTER key.

____   If necessary, scroll to display the desired clip art. Click the desired clip art.

____   Click the Insert clip button on the Pop-up menu.

____   Position the mouse pointer anywhere within the clip art region of the Object Area placeholder and double-click.

____   Click the Search for clips text box and type the keywords.

Short Answer (5)

Write a brief answer to each question.

1. Why would you want to change the view from slide view to outline view when you are designing a presentation? When are outlines used in presentations?

2. Where would you obtain clip art for a PowerPoint presentation? Besides having a wide variety of clip art images, the Microsoft Clip Gallery 5.0 contains what other components?

3. How do slide transition effects differ from custom animation effects? When would you use each in your presentations?

4. When would you want to do a fast save? A full save? How do you change from one saving method to another?

5. How does the information in a header differ from that in a footer? Why would you want to use headers and footers in your presentations?

Activities

Use Help

Use Help to answer each question.

1. How do you **change the information on a header or footer**, such as the date, time, or slide number? Use the Office Assistant to find out.

2. What are some **computer-based slideshow design guidelines**? Look in the Designing Slide Shows book on the Contents sheet to find out.

3. How can you add **music, sounds, videos, and animated GIF pictures to your presentation**? Use the Index sheet to find out.

Expanding on the Lab

Perform the following tasks.

1. Open the SAD presentation created in In the Lab 1.

2. Change the title of Slide 1 to Winter Blues or SAD?. Italicize your name on the slide. Add today's date to the outline header and the slide number to the outline footer.

3. On Slide 2, substitute the clip art that has the keywords, blue moons unhappiness sadness. Increase the bulleted list line spacing to 0.3 lines before each paragraph.

4. On Slide 4, substitute the clip art that has the keywords, happiness joy laughing facial expressions excitement.

5. On Slides 2, 3, and 4, italicize the titles Symptoms of SAD, Causes of SAD, and Relief for SAD. Change the font size to 40 points.

6. Apply the Checkerboard Across slide transition effect to all slides. Apply the Blinds Vertical custom animation effect to all heading level 1 paragraphs on Slides 2 and 3.

7. Check the presentation for errors.

8. Print the revised presentation outline. Print the revised black and white presentation.

9. Quit PowerPoint without saving the revised presentation.

Puzzle

Use the clues below to complete the word search puzzle. Words in the puzzle may be forward or backward, across, up and down, or diagonal.

Using Outline View

```
N  P  R  O  M  O  T  E  ▣  I  O  T  F  ▣  F
O  ▣  W  U  S  ▣  ▣  D  ▣  N  I  R  O  T  D
I  ▣  E  T  U  ▣  P  I  S  F  T  A  R  T  E
T  ▣  I  L  B  S  O  L  K  O  A  P  M  U  M
A  ▣  V  I  O  I  R  S  N  R  R  I  A  O  O
M  F  E  N  R  Z  D  Y  I  M  T  L  T  Y  T
I  O  N  E  D  E  D  R  L  A  C  C  P  A  E
N  O  I  T  I  S  N  A  R  T  E  D  I  L  S
A  T  L  I  N  H  A  M  E  I  P  N  C  E  P
M  E  T  T  A  E  G  M  P  O  S  A  T  D  A
O  R  U  L  T  E  A  U  Y  N  A  P  U  I  L
T  C  O  E  E  T  R  S  H  A  K  X  R  L  L
S  ▣  ▣  H  E  A  D  E  R  L  C  E  E  S  O
U  S  K  S  A  T  N  O  M  M  O  C  ▣  ▣  C
C  D  R  A  O  B  N  I  T  E  L  L  U  B  ▣
```

The subject of the presentation.

Provides a quick, easy way to create a presentation.

A summary of thoughts, presented as headings and subheadings, often used as a preliminary draft when creating a presentation.

File extension that stands for Rich Text Format.

Outlining toolbar button that moves a selected paragraph to the next-higher heading level.

Outlining toolbar button that moves a selected paragraph to the next-lower heading level.

Outlining toolbar button that hides all but the title of selected slides.

Outlining toolbar button that displays the titles and collapsed text of selected slides.

Outlining toolbar button that creates a new slide from the slides selected in slide sorter or normal view.

Used to change the order of text or slides.

Type of slide that introduces the main topic.

Type of slides that support the main topic.

After a slide is created, the button used to change a its layout.

Dialog box that allows you to choose one of 24 different AutoLayouts.

Offers a quick way to add professional-looking graphic images to a presentation.

System that allows computer users to communicate with each other and share files.

Command used to change the size of a clip art picture by an exact percentage.

Contains options for changing the size of a picture.

Check box that, when it contains a check mark, changes height and width settings to maintain the aspect ration of the original picture.

The relationship between the height and width of an object.

Shortcuts that allow a user to jump from a presentation to another destination.

Special effect used to progress from one slide to the next in a show.

Effects that define animation types and speeds and sound effects on a slide.

Displays at the top of a sheet of paper or slide.

Displays at the bottom of a sheet of paper or slide.

Microsoft PowerPoint 2000
Web Feature
Creating a Presentation on the Web Using PowerPoint

Overview

This Web feature illustrates creating a Web page by saving an existing PowerPoint presentation as an HTML file. You learn how to view the presentation as a Web page in your default browser. Then you modify a slide and view that modified slide using your default browser. Once the presentation is converted to a Web page, you can post the file to an intranet or to the World Wide Web.

Project Outline

I. Introduction [PPW 1.1]

  An intranet is _____

  You need an FTP (File Transfer Protocol) program to _____

  _____

  The AutoContent Wizard provides _____

  The Save as Web Page command allows you to _____

II. Saving a PowerPoint presentation as a Web page [PPW 1.3]

  To publish a presentation means to _____

  ☞ To save a PowerPoint presentation as a Web page:

    1. _____

    2. _____

    3. _____

    4. _____

  A custom show is _____

  A check mark in the Display speaker notes check box in the Publish what? area of the Publish as

  Web Page dialog box should be removed if_____

III. Viewing a presentation as a Web page [PPW 1.6]

  The Expand/Collapse Outline button allows you to_____

☞   To view a presentation as a Web page

1. _____

2. _____

3. _____

4. _____

5. _____

The Show/Hide Outline button allows you to _____

The Show/Hide Notes button allows you to _____

The Next Slide button allows you to _____

The Previous slide button allows you to _____

IV.   Editing a web page through a browser [PPW 1.9]

☞   To edit a Web page through a browser

1. _____

2. _____

3. _____

4. _____

5. _____

Clicking the Refresh button displays _____

6. _____

7. _____

Review

Matching (5)

Match each term on the left with the best description from the right.

___ 1. ISP

___ 2. AutoContent Wizard

___ 3. publish

a. creates a subset of your presentation that contains slides tailored for a specific audience

b. provides designs and content ideas to help you develop a slide show for the Internet

c. to design a Web page

d. to save Web pages to a Web folder or an FTP location

e. the computer to which you post files for publication on a Web page

True/False (5)

*Circle **T** if the statement is true and **F** if the statement is false.*

T F 1. The presentation pane lets you type speaker notes to remind you of information you want to share with your audience.

T F 2. The Save as Web Page command allows you to create a Web page from a single slide or a from a multiple-slide presentation.

T F 3. An Internet is an internal network that uses Web technologies.

T F 4. You can alter the browser window by choosing to display or hide the outline and notes panes.

T F 5. A micro show is a subset of your presentation that contains slides tailored for a specific audience.

Fill in the Blanks (3)

Write a word (or words) on the blank to correctly complete each sentence.

1. A company's _____ is an internal network that uses Internet technologies.

2. PowerPoint provides a Web presentation template in the _____ option when you start PowerPoint.

3. A(n) _____ is a subset of your presentation that contains slides tailored for a specific audience.

Multiple Choice (2)

Circle the letter of the best answer.

1. Which of the following is a way to use PowerPoint to create Web pages?
   a. using the Web Presentation template in the AutoContent Wizard
   b. using the Save as Web Page command
   c. using the Save as Web Page command
   d. all of the above

2. Which browser button displays the most current version of a Web page?
   a. Restore
   b. Newest
   c. Load
   d. Refresh

The Microsoft Internet Explorer Window (5)

Identify the elements indicated in Figure PP5.

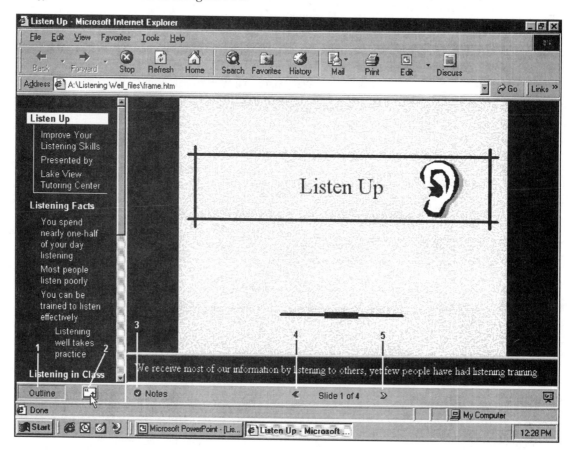

Figure PP5

1. _____   4. _____

2. _____   5. _____

3. _____

Short Answer (2)

Write a brief answer to each question.

1. What are the three ways to create a Web page using PowerPoint?

2. What is the function of the PowerPoint Viewer?

Activities

Use Help

Use Help to answer each question.

1. How do you **access the Office Update home page**? What information can you get there? Use the Office Assistant to find out.

2. How do you **update a Web presentation after you publish it**? Look in the Publishing to the Web book in the Working with Presentations on Intranets and the Internet book on the Contents sheet to find out.

Expanding on the Lab

Perform the following tasks.

1. Open the Scholarship Sources presentation created in In the Lab 2 in the Web feature.

2. View the presentation in a browser.

3. Switch the order of Slides 2 and 3.

4. Modify Slide 4 by adding a third First level paragraph beneath Personal income not considered that says Available for a wide variety of talents and activities.

5. View the modified pages in a browser.

6. Ask your instructor for instructions on how to post your Web page so others may have access to it.

Microsoft Outlook 2000

Project One
Schedule and Contact Management
Using Outlook

Overview

This project illustrates using Outlook to create a personal schedule, task list, and a contact list. You learn how to enter appointments, create recurring appointments, move appointments to new dates, schedule events, and view and print your calendar in different views and print styles. You create a task list to serve as a reminder of tasks to be completed. You also create and print a contact list. Finally, you export your personal subfolders onto a floppy disk and later import the subfolders for further updating.

Project Outline

   I. What is Microsoft Outlook 2000? [O 1.6]

      Microsoft Outlook 2000 is _____

      A desktop information management program is _____

  II. Project One – Tamara Wilson's DIM System [O 1.6]

 III. Starting Outlook [O 1.8]

      ☞ To start Outlook

         1. _____

      Outlook items include _____

      The information viewer displays _____

      When a folder is opened _____

      A. Opening the Calendar folder [O 1.8]

        ☞ To open the Calendar folder

           1. _____

              Day view allows you to _____

           2. _____

 IV. The Calendar – Microsoft Outlook window [O 1.9]

      The Calendar – Microsoft Outlook window includes _____

      _____

Features of the Calendar – Microsoft Outlook window:

- Folder banner _____
- Date Navigator _____
- Appointment area _____

  An appointment is _____

  A meeting is _____

  An event is _____

- TaskPad _____

  Tasks are _____

  Double-click the Tasks shortcut to _____

  Select the check box in the Complete column to _____

- Outlook Shortcuts _____

  The Outlook bar contains _____

- My Shortcuts _____
- Other Shortcuts _____
- Standard toolbar _____

A. Creating a personal subfolder in the Calendar folder [O 1.11]

☞ To create a personal subfolder in the Calendar folder

   1. _____

   2. _____

   3. _____

   A plus sign next to a folder indicates _____

   A minus sign next to a folder indicates _____

☞ To change to a personal folder

   1. _____

V. Entering appointments using the appointment area [O 1.13]

☞ To enter appointments using the appointment area

   1. _____

   2. _____

       _____

   3. _____

   4. _____

   5. _____

Press the ENTER key or click outside the appointment time slot to complete the appointment.

If you notice an error before pressing the ENTER key, use the BACKSPACE key to _____
_____

Press the ESC key to _____

A. Entering appointments using the Appointment window [O 1.15]

You can use the Appointment window to _____

☞ To enter and save appointments using the Appointment window

    1. _____

    2. _____

    3. _____

The Reminder symbol is _____

Press the TAB key to _____

B. Recurring appointments [O 1.17]

Recurring appointments are _____

☞ To set recurring appointments

    1. _____
      _____

    2. _____

    The Recurrence symbol displays _____

    3. _____
      _____

    4. _____

    5. _____

The Format View command allows you to _____

C. Moving to the next day in Calendar [O 1.19]

☞ To move to the next day in the Appointment area

    1. _____
      _____

    2. _____

☞ To complete the recurring appointments

    1. _____

The No end date option button is used when _____

D. Using natural language phrases to enter appointment dates and times [O 1.20]

The AutoDate function is used to _____

☞ To enter appointment dates and times using natural language phrases:

    1. _____

    2. _____

3. _____

4. _____

5. _____

VI. Editing appointments [O 1.23]

   A. Deleting appointments [O 1.23]

     ☞ To delete an appointment

       1. _____

       2. _____

       3. _____

       4. _____

VII. Moving appointments to a new time [O 1.24]

     ☞ To move an appointment to a new time

       1. _____

       2. _____

       3. _____

          The drag icon is _____

       4. _____

VIII. Moving appointments to a new date [O 1.26]

     ☞ To move an appointment to a new date

       1. _____

          _____

       2. _____

IX. Moving an appointment to a new month [O 1.27]

     ☞ To move an appointment to a new month

       1. _____

          _____

       2. _____

       3. _____

       4. _____

X. Creating an event [O 1.29]

   An event is _____

   A small banner displays _____

     ☞ To create an event

       1. _____

2. _____

3. _____

XI. Displaying the Calendar in Week and Month views [O 1.30]

While in Day/Week/Month view, Outlook can _____

_____

A. Work Week view [O 1.30]

Work week view shows _____

☞ To change to Work Week view

1. _____

B. Week view [O 1.31]

Week view shows _____

☞ To change to Work Week view

1. _____

C. Month view [O 1.32]

Month view resembles_____

☞ To change to Month view

1. _____

2. _____

XII. Creating a task list using the TaskPad [O 1.33]

A task is _____

The task list is_____

The TaskPad is used to _____

☞ To create a task list using the TaskPad

1. _____

2. _____

3. _____

4. _____

5. _____

A Completed icon displays _____

To add details to tasks _____

XIII. Printing a calendar [O 1.35]

Print styles are _____

A. Daily Style [O 1.35]

Daily Style shows _____

☞   To print the calendar in Daily Style:

1. _____

2. _____

The Daily Style printout includes _____

_____

The Page Setup button allows _____

B.   Weekly Style [O 1.36]

☞   To print the calendar in Weekly Style

1. _____

_____

C.   Monthly Style [O 1.36]

☞   To print the calendar in Monthly Style

1. _____

_____

Tri-fold Style prints_____

Use the Define Styles button to _____

D.   Printing the Task List [O 1.36]

☞   To print the task list

1. _____

2. _____

XIV.   Contacts [O 1.37]

A contact is _____

The Contacts component of Outlook allows you to store _____

A contact list is_____

•   The Find option allows you to _____

Address Card view displays _____

A.   Creating a personal subfolder in the Contacts folder [O 1.38]

☞   To create a personal subfolder in the Contacts folder

1. _____

_____

2. _____

3. _____

4. _____

B. Creating a contact list [O 1.39]

☞ To create a contact list

1. _____

2. _____

3. _____

    _____

4. _____

5. _____

Clicking the Details tab allows you to _____

C. Finding a contact quickly [O 1.42]

Use the Find a Contact box to _____

☞ To find a contact quickly

1. _____

2. _____

3. _____

D. Organizing contacts [O 1.43]

☞ To organize contacts

1. _____

2. _____

3. _____

4. _____

E. Printing the contact list [O 1.45]

☞ To print the contact list

1. _____

XV. Exporting, deleting, and importing subfolders [O 1.46]

The Import and Export Wizard is used to _____

The extension .pst indicates _____

• Exporting is _____

• Importing is _____

A. Exporting subfolders [O 1.46]

☞ To export subfolders onto a floppy disk

1. _____

2. _____

3. _____

    _____

4. _____

5. _____

6. _____

7. _____

_____

_____

B.   Deleting subfolders [O 1.48]

☞   To delete a personal subfolder

1. _____

2. _____

3. _____

_____

4. _____

C.   Importing subfolders [O 1.50]

☞   To import a subfolder

1. _____

_____

_____

XVI.   Quitting Outlook [O 1.51]

☞   To quit Outlook

1. _____

Review

Matching (5)

Match each term on the left with the best description from the right.

___ 1. TaskPad

___ 2. Monthly Style

___ 3. Subfolder

___ 4. Folder List

___ 5. AutoDate function

a. one of the ways to print a calendar

b. a display available on the View menu to show folders and subfolders

c. a two-month view of the calendar

d. an Outlook folder for personal use

e. a view of the things you need to see done through completion

f. a one-time, all day event

g. the ability to use natural language phrases such as "Next Tuesday" instead of the actual numeric date

True/False (10)

*Circle **T** if the statement is true and **F** if the statement is false.*

T F 1. The Calendar folder is located on the Outlook Bar.

T F 2. The Date Navigator typically shows a two-month calendar.

T F 3. Appointments and events are entered the same way.

T F 4. Appointments can recur any number of days per week.

T F 5. Dragging an appointment to the Date Navigator moves the appointment to a new date.

T F 6. Entering a task automatically creates an appointment.

T F 7. The Event banner is located on the Outlook Bar.

T F 8. The Contacts window allows multiple e-mail addresses.

T F 9. If your computer is online with an Internet provider, clicking a contact's home page in the Contact window automatically will pull up that page.

T F 10. Contacts can only be ordered alphabetically by last name.

Definitions (5)

Briefly define each term.

1. appointment _____

2. event _____

3. recurrence _____

4. task _____

5. contact _____

The Outlook Screen (5)

Identify the elements indicated in Figure O1.

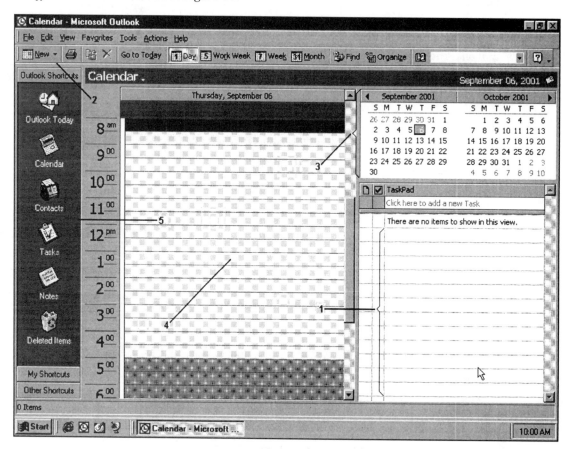

Figure O1

1. _____   4. _____

2. _____   5. _____

3. _____

Multiple Choice (5)

Circle the letter of the best answer.

1. Why is it important to create a personal subfolder of the Calendar folder rather than enter your data into the Calendar folder itself?
   a. several people may work on the same computer
   b. you may keep several people's schedules
   c. it makes it easier to import and export the folders of data
   d. all of the above

2. What is the easiest way to move an appointment to a new time on the same day?
   a. drag it to the Date Navigator
   b. drag it to the new time slot
   c. open the appointment window and change the time
   d. cut and paste

3. What kind of entry would you make for a holiday?
   a. an appointment
   b. a recurring appointment, yearly
   c. an event
   d. a task

4. Which of the following is *not* entered on any tab in the Contacts window?
   a. business telephone
   b. nickname
   c. home page URL
   d. name of the person who referred the contact

5. What does a check mark mean to the left of a task in the TaskPad?
   a. the task is completed
   b. the task has been assigned to someone else
   c. the task is current
   d. the task has been moved to an appointment

Dialog Box (5)

Answer the following questions about the Appointment Recurrence dialog box in Figure O2.

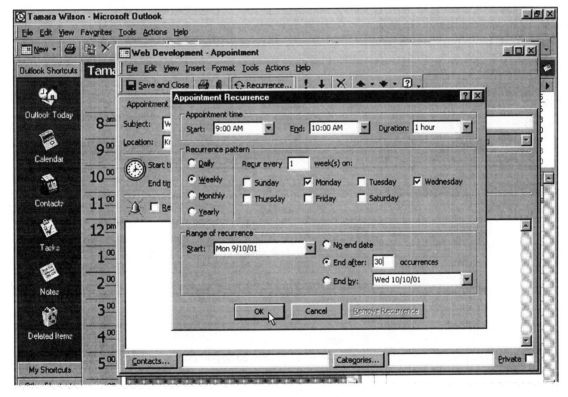

Figure O2

1. How was the dialog box displayed?_____

2. How often is the recurrence? _____

3. How long is the appointment?_____

4. When will the recurrence end? _____

5. How would you complete the recurrence? _____

Fill in the Blanks (5)

Write a word (or words) in the blank to complete each sentence correctly.

1. You can print all or part of your calendar in a number of different layouts or _____.

2. If you have a long list of contacts, use the _____ on the Standard toolbar to locate a specific contact by last name.

3. To move, copy, or delete a subfolder, _____ the folder name in the Folder List to pull up the shortcut menu.

4. The Import and Export command is located on the _____ menu.

5. On the Standard toolbar, the button with the number 7 on it displays the calendar in _____.

Sequence (5)

Use the numbers 1 – 5 to show the order in which these steps should be performed to print a calendar in Weekly Style.

____   Select the date in the Date Navigator.

____   Ready the printer.

____   Click the Print button.

____   Click OK.

____   Click Weekly Style.

Short Answer (5)

Write a brief answer to each question.

1. How is an event different from an all-day appointment?

2. Why might it be easier to enter "a week from today" instead of the exact date?

3. When would you use the cut-and-paste method to move an appointment?

4. What is the Import and Export Wizard and why is it useful in Outlook?

5.   Why are some dates displayed in bold on the Date Navigator?

Activities

Use Help

Use Help to answer each question.

1. How do you **find an appointment** quickly in a large calendar? Use the Office Assistant to find out.

2. How do you **turn off the reminder sound**? Use the Office Assistant to find out.

3. How do you **look at the Calendar and Contact windows at the same time**? Use the Office Assistant to find out.

Expanding on the Lab

Perform the following tasks.

1. Import the My Schedule subfolder you created in In the Lab 1.

2. Delete the haircut appointment on February 6.

3. Schedule the Homecoming parade for noon on October 1.

4. Add a task in the TaskPad to remind you to finish the paper for your English literature class.

5. Print your schedule for the week including January 11.

6. Export your subfolder back to your floppy disk and then delete it from the hard disk.

Puzzle

Use the clues given to complete the crossword puzzle.

Schedule and Contact Management

Down

1. Print style that shows a day's appointments, tasks, and a two-month calendar.
2. Key used to move through fields in the Appointment window.
3. Bell icon that displays next to appointments with reminders.
4. An activity that does not involve other resources or people.
5. Displays items in the selected folder.
6. Roster of important contact information.
7. In the Contacts window, clicked to enter a contact's department, nickname, or birthday.
9. Print style that produces a daily appointment list, a task list, and a calendar for the week.
10. Shows Monday through Friday in columnar style.
11. Shows how many appointments are scheduled for any given week.
13. Personal or work-related duties that need to be tracked.
15. Indicates a folder is expanded.
17. Outlook function that provides the capability of specifying dates and times using natural language phrases.
19. Outlook option that lets you search for a contact name in your address book.
21. Extension Outlook uses when saving subfolders.

Across

1. Includes two monthly calendars and scroll arrows.
8. Displays next to a finished task.
12. Contains a date heading and time slots for the current view.
14. Outlook component that allows you to store information about individuals or companies.
16. Transferring a subfolder onto a floppy disk.
18. Roster of items that need to be tracked through completion.
20. Displays your schedule for an entire month.
22. Displays your tasks and their status.
23. Moving a subfolder back to a computer.
24. An appointment to which other resources or people are invited.

Microsoft Office 2000 Integration

Project One
Integrating Office 2000 Applications and the World Wide Web

Overview

This project illustrates the integration of Microsoft Office 2000 applications. You begin the project by opening an existing Word document and creating a two-column, one-row, borderless table. You then learn how to insert three hyperlinks and embed a 3-D Pie chart from an existing Excel worksheet. You save that document as an HTML file. You then open an existing PowerPoint presentation and add a hyperlink to the first slide. You save this presentation as a Web page. You open an existing Access database. You use the Wizard to create a data access page from that database. You create a group structure so that the database could be viewed but not changed. Finally, you save that data access page and view and test all Web pages and hyperlinks in your browser.

Project Outline

I. Introduction [I 1.4]

With the Web page creation capabilities of Office 2000, an entire Web site can be created by integrating a Word document that contains a company logo and company name, an Excel workbook that contains a 3-D Pie chart graphically illustrating the company's breakdown by product, a PowerPoint slideshow that contains general company information, and an Access database that contains product information.

II. Integration Project – Global Computers Web site [I 1.5]

III. Adding hyperlinks to a Word document [I 1.5]

A home page is _____

A hyperlink is _____

☞ To start Word and open an existing document

1. _____

2. _____

3. _____

4. _____

5. _____

A. Inserting a table into a Word document [I 1.8]

☞ To insert a table into a Word document

1. _____

   _____

2. _____

   _____

3. _____

The AutoFit to contents option allows you to _____

_____

B. Eliminating the table border [I 1.10]

☞ To remove the table border

1. _____

   _____

2. _____

   _____

C. Inserting the text for the hyperlinks [I 1.11]

☞ To insert text for hyperlinks

1. _____

2. _____

   _____

D. Inserting a hyperlink to PowerPoint Web pages [I 1.12]

The Insert Hyperlink feature provides the capability of _____

_____

☞ To insert a hyperlink to PowerPoint Web pages

1. _____

2. _____

   _____

3. _____

☞ To insert the remaining hyperlinks

1. _____

2. _____

3. _____

4. _____

IV. Embedding an Excel chart into a Word document [I 1.13]

Object Linking and Embedding (OLE) allows you to _____

A source object is _____

A destination object is _____

The Paste Special command allows you to _____

The source program is _____

☞ To open an Excel workbook

    1. _____

    2. _____

    3. _____

    4. _____

☞ To embed an Excel chart into a Word document

    1. _____

    2. _____

    3. _____

    4. _____

    5. _____

    6. _____

Three methods can be used to copy objects between Microsoft Office applications.

Copy Methods	
METHOD	*CHARACTERISTICS*
Copy and paste	_____ _____
Copy and embed	_____ _____ _____
Copy and link	_____ _____ _____

A. Changing the size of an embedded object [I 1.16]

    ☞ To change the size of an embedded object

        1. _____

        2. _____

        3. _____

        4. _____

The Size and rotate area of the Format Object dialog box allows you to _____

_____

The Scale area of the Format Object dialog box allows you to _____

_____

The Original size area displays _____

The aspect ratio of an object is _____

    B. Quitting Excel [I 1.19]

      ☞ To quit Excel

        1. _____

        2. _____

V. Adding scrolling text to a Word document [I 1.20]

A scrolling marquee is _____

The Scrolling Text button is used to_____

  ☞ To display the Web Tools toolbar

      1. _____

      2. _____

    A. Inserting scrolling text [I 1.21]

The behavior of text _____

Scrolling moves the text _____

Setting text's behavior to slide moves _____

Setting text's behavior to alternate moves _____

      ☞ To insert scrolling text

        1. _____

            _____

        2. _____

        3. _____

        4. _____

The direction of text movement can be _____

The speed of text movement can be _____

The background attribute determines _____

The loop attribute determines _____

    B. Resizing the scrolling text [I 1.22]

      ☞ To resize the scrolling text

        1. _____

        2. _____

3. _____

4. _____

VI. Viewing the Word document in your browser and saving it as a Web page [I 1.24]

☞ To preview the Web page

1. _____

2. _____

3. _____

☞ To save a document with a new file name

1. _____

2. _____

3. _____

4. _____

HTML is _____

☞ To quit Word

1. _____

VII. Creating a PowerPoint presentation Web page [I 1.26]

You can create Web pages from an existing PowerPoint presentation using _____

_____

☞ To open a PowerPoint presentation

1. _____

2. _____

3. _____

A. Adding text for a hyperlink [I 1.27]

☞ To add text for a hyperlink

1. _____

2. _____

3. _____

B. Creating a hyperlink [I 1.28]

☞ To create a hyperlink in a PowerPoint presentation

1. _____

2. _____

3. _____

4. _____

C. Viewing and saving the PowerPoint Web page [I 1.29]

☞ To view the Web page in your browser

1. _____

2. _____

3. _____

In PowerPoint, the outline is _____

The Expand/Collapse Outline button is used to _____

Action buttons _____

D. Saving the PowerPoint presentation as a Web page [I 1.31]

☞ To save the PowerPoint presentation as a Web page

1. _____

2. _____

3. _____

4. _____

5. _____

☞ To quit PowerPoint and close your browser

1. _____

2. _____

VIII. Creating a data access page from an Access database [I 1.31]

A data access page is _____

☞ To open an Access database

1. _____

2. _____

3. _____

A. Creating a data access page using the wizard [I 1.32]

Adding group levels results in _____

☞ To create a data access page using the wizard

1. _____

2. _____

3. _____

4. _____

5. _____

6. _____

7. _____

B. Adding a title and image to a data access page [I 1.36]

☞ To add a title and image to a data access page

1. _____

2. _____

3. _____

4. _____

5. _____

C. Adding a hyperlink to a data access page [I 1.37]

☞ To add a hyperlink to a data access page

1. _____

2. _____

3. _____

4. _____

D. Saving the data access page and viewing it [I 1.39]

☞ To save the data access page and view it in your browser

1. _____

2. _____

3. _____

4. _____

☞ To quit Access and close your browser

1. _____

2. _____

Record navigation toolbars are used to _____

IX. Testing the Web site [I 1.40]

☞ To test the Web site

1. _____

2. _____

3. _____

A. Verifying the hyperlinks in your browser [I 1.41]

☞ To verify the hyperlinks

1. _____

2. _____

3. _____

4. _____

5. _____

6. _____

☞ To quit e-mail and close your browser:

1. _____

2. _____

Review

Matching (5)

Match each term on the left with the best description from the right.

___ 1. linking

___ 2. alternate

___ 3. slide master

___ 4. slide

___ 5. Insert Hyperlink feature

a. copy method in which the source document does not become part of the destination document

b. provides the capability of linking to a Web page

c. scrolling text behavior that bounces the text back and forth in the marquee's margins

d. feature used to insert action buttons

e. scrolling text behavior that moves the text from one side of the Web page and stops as soon as it touches the opposite side

f. used to navigate through a Web page presentation

g. changes the size of an object by specifying a percentage

True/False (10)

*Circle **T** if the statement is true and **F** if the statement is false.*

T F 1. You can group and edit data on a data access page.

T F 2. Adding group levels to a data access page results in a read-only page.

T F 3. Expandable buttons contain shapes, such as left and right arrows, that can be used to hyperlink to other Web pages within a presentation.

T F 4. PowerPoint 2000 allows you to create Web pages from an existing PowerPoint presentation, using the FTP to ISP feature.

T F 5. HTML is a programming language used for Web page creation.

T F 6. Saving a Word document as an FTP file makes it possible for it to be viewed using a browser such as Internet Explorer.

T F 7. The loop attribute of scrolling text determines the number of times that the scrolling text moves across the Web page.

T F 8. A scrolling banner is a line of text that moves from one side of the Web page to another.

T F 9. When you embed an object, the object may be edited in the destination document using source editing features.

T F 10. When you attempt to edit a linked worksheet in Word, the system activates Excel.

Definitions (5)

Briefly define each term.

1. behavior (of scrolling text) _____

2. aspect ratio _____

3. destination document _____

4. hyperlink _____

5. source object _____

The Integration Screen (5)

Identify the elements indicated in Figure I1.

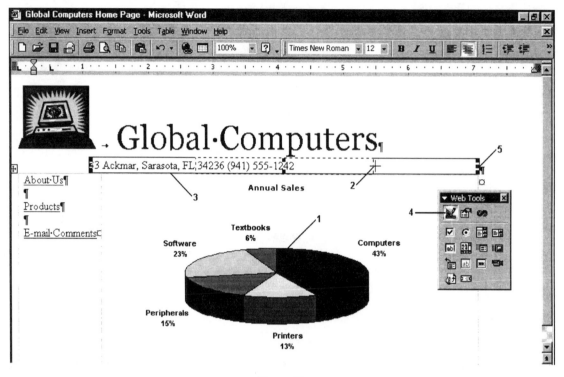

Figure I1

1. _____   4. _____

2. _____   5. _____

3. _____

Multiple Choice (5)

Circle the letter of the best answer.

1. Which of the following is a programming language used for Web page creation?
   a. ISP
   b. HTML
   c. Access
   d. Marquee

2. Which Microsoft Office 2000 feature allows you to insert an Excel chart into a Word document?
   a. datatbinding
   b. OLE
   c. HTML
   d. hyperlinking

3. Why are data access pages used?
   a. to analyze data
   b. to review data
   c. to enter and edit data
   d. all of the above

4. In which of the following copy methods does the source document NOT become part of the destination document?
   a. pasting
   b. linking
   c. embedding
   d. all of the above

5. Which Edit menu command do you use to embed an object?
   a. Paste
   b. Paste Special
   c. Embed
   d. Insert

Dialog Box (5)

Answer the following questions about the Format Object dialog box shown in Figure I2.

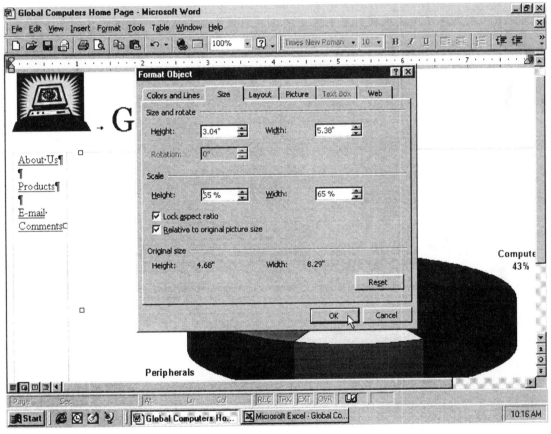

Figure I2

1. How was the dialog box displayed?_____

2. Which sheet is selected? _____

3. What was the original size of the object? _____

4. If you change the height, what other value would change? _____

5. How would you exit this dialog box? _____

Fill in the Blanks (5)

Write a word (or words) in the blank to complete each sentence correctly.

1. The _____ option in the Insert Table dialog box allows you to make the columns in a table automatically adjust to fit the contents.

2. To copy and paste text as a hyperlink, copy the text you want to the _____, click where you want to insert the text, and then click Paste as Hyperlink on the Edit menu.

3. The _____ dialog box contains two areas with which to change the size of an object.

4. With Word 2000, you can create scrolling text using the Scrolling Text button on the _____ toolbar.

5. Outline pane is displayed by default when you view a presentation in a(n) _____.

Sequence (5)

Use the numbers 1 – 5 to show the order in which these steps should be performed to change the size of an embedded object.

____   Click OK to finish the resizing.

____   Change the height or width in the Scale area.

____   Click Object and then click Size.

____   Click Format on the menu bar.

____   Click the object to select it.

Short Answer (5)

Write a brief answer to each question.

1. What is the difference between source and destination files when embedding?

2. What is a data access page? How is it similar to a form?

3. What is the difference between linking and embedding an object?

4. What is the behavior of scrolling text? Provide some examples.

5. What is the advantage of using an integrated set of applications like Microsoft Office 2000?

Activities

Use Help

Use Help to answer each question.

1. How do **you insert a PowerPoint slide into a Word document**? Use the Index sheet to find out.

2. How do you **embed or create hyperlinks** when working with online or Internet document? Look in the Working with Hyperlinks book in the Working with Online and Internet Documents book on the Contents sheet to find out.

3. How do you **insert the contents of a Microsoft Access table or query into an existing Word document**? Use the Office Assistant to find out.

Expanding on the Lab

Perform the following tasks.

1. Use Word to open the SSI.htm file you created in In the Lab 1.

2. Reduce the size of the embedded Excel Worksheet Object to 75% its current height and 50% its current width.

3. Add a third column to the centered, borderless table at the bottom of the page and add the hyperlink with the text Search the Internet. This hyperlink should jump to the Web page www.yahoo.com.

4. Save this file as NEWSSI.htm.

5. View the NEWSSI.htm file in your browser. Print the Web page.

Puzzle

The terms described by the phrases below are written below each line in code. Break the code by writing the correct term above the coded word. Then, use your broken code to translate the final sentence.

1. Allows you to make the columns in a table automatically fit the contents.

   XRQLCFQ QL ZLKQBKQP

2. Once a document is embedded, it becomes part of this document.

   ABPQFKXQFLK

3. This Format Object dialog box area allows you to change the size of an object by a specific percentage.

   PZXIB

4. The size area at the bottom of the Format Object dialog box.

   LOFDFKXI

5. This attribute of text specifies the manner in which this text moves on the Web page.

   YBEXSFLO

6. This attribute of text determines the number of times that the scrolling text moves across the page.

   ILLM

7. HTML is used for the creation of these.

   TBY MXDBP

8. Allows you to create Web pages from an existing PowerPoint presentation, using the Save as Web Page feature.

   MLTBOMLFKQ 7666

9. A special type of Web page designed for viewing and working with data.

   AXQX XZZBPP MXDB

XK BKQFOB TBY PFGB ZXK YB ZOBXQBA TFOE LCCFZB 7666 CFIBP, RPFKD QEB

PXSB XP TBY MXDB CBXQROB.

Notes